Flash Nonfiction Funny

71 Very Humorous, Very True, Very Short Stories

FLASH
Nonfiction
FUNNY

71 Very Humorous,
VERY TRUE,
Very Short Stories

Edited by
Tom Hazuka *and* **Dinty W. Moore**

woodhall press
NORWALK, CONNECTICUT

Library of Congress Cataloguing-in-Publication Data available

978-0-9975437-4-2, paperback
978-0-9975437-5-9, ebook

First Edition

This book is dedicated to our long-suffering wives,

Christine Perkins-Hazuka and Renita M. Romasco,

for putting up with our quixotic literary antics.

This is a book of flash nonfiction. Each author has created
a complete story in 750 words or fewer. Some pieces experiment
with form, others take a more traditional approach,
but all of them celebrate the precise and concise style of writing that
inspired Shakespeare to call brevity the soul of wit.

Preface

This book has been years in the making. Shortly after my anthology *Flash Fiction Funny* was born in 2013, I began thinking it could use a nonfiction sibling. Although I was pretty sure *Flash Fiction Funny* realized people were laughing *with* it, not *at* it, I figured that a jolly companion would be a boost to its psyche, and possibly to its self-esteem as well. At the very least, I hoped *Flash Fiction Funny* would learn to play well with others.

I had made a questionable decision to be a single parent with *Flash Fiction Funny*, the only one of my eight anthologies that I edited solo, and I definitely wanted a partner to raise this new baby. But who? After minimal cogitation (my favorite kind), I hit upon the name of Dinty W. Moore, founder and editor of *Brevity* magazine, the gold standard for flash nonfiction.

I had little trouble locating Dinty. Also, in the interest of strict honesty (this being a nonfiction preface), because his story "Revolution" is in *Flash Fiction Funny* I already had his address. I emailed Dinty about coediting *Flash Nonfiction Funny*.

Dinty could hardly contain his excitement. Scarcely three months later he responded. I will quote his exuberant response in its entirety: "I guess . . .". He had obviously intended to use three exclamation points but, inspired by the ghost of Rosemary Woods, had made an entirely understandable mistake, given the proximity of the period and the exclamation point on a keyboard.

OK, I admit that the previous paragraph was not strictly nonfiction. In fact, I totally invented that version. The truth is that Dinty responded right away, with only one question: What did I mean by the term "coeditor"? I assured him that we would share equally in the wealth and the glory.

"You mean the hassles and the headaches?" he responded. "For far less than minimum wage?" He added a smiley emoji, and a winking emoticon for emphasis.

Ah, yes, I realized, this is a kindred spirit with vast editorial experience and insight, and our labor of love is destined to join the literary pantheon.

"Dinty," I typed back with a blazing two fingers. "I think this is the beginning of a beautiful friendship—or at least a reasonably civil working relationship."

I smiled hysterically at how warm and fuzzy I felt. In a good way.

So Dinty joined me as both midwife and parent to this child, and fortunately he turned out to be a stricter disciplinarian than I am. Despite some youthful indiscretions, *Flash Nonfiction Funny* managed to stay out of jail and promises to be an at least semiproductive member of society.

I'm sure I speak for Dinty when I say: We're proud of you, kid.

—TOM HAZUKA

I remember well the April morning Tom Hazuka reached out to me, my initial horror, my finger hovering over the e-mail, my lizard brain hissing "delete, delete, delete."

But Mom raised me to be polite, so I responded, "I guess . . .", and then sent him my list of demands:

1. You do all the work.

2. Contact me only on the third Tuesday of the month, before noon, but not if the month ends in a "y."

3. Don't expect me to answer.

4. My name goes first on the cover. (Alphabetically, Dinty comes before Tom.)

I was counting, of course, on the project going belly-up within months. After all, who writes funny-but-true stories under a 750-word limit? One poor loser with no real literary life? Maybe two?

Soon, however, submissions for *Flash Nonfiction Funny* began rolling in, like a scene from the movie *Titanic*, but without the sappy music, and it became painfully clear that the book would likely someday see the light of day. It was around this point that I insisted my name *not* be on the cover.

The result of Tom's hard work, and my horrible disposition, is the book you now hold in your hands. (By the way, if you are standing in a bookstore reading this preface, please pay for the book *before* getting greasy fingerprints all over the pages.)

I hope you enjoy our little bundle of flash nonfiction joy. Goodness knows, Tom and I have cherished every bitter moment of our brief but reluctant editorial collaboration.

—DINTY W. MOORE

Table of Contents

Stuff the Dog Ate

BRIAN DOYLE

One: Ancient squashed dried round flat shard of beaver! Sweet mother of the mewling baby Jesus! You wouldn't think a creature who likes to watch Peter O'Toole movies would be such an omnivorous gobbling machine, but he has eaten everything from wasps to the back half of a raccoon one time. But let us not ignore the beaver. Speculation is that beaver was washed up onto the road when the overflowing lake blew its dam, was squashed by a truck, and then got flattened ten thousand times more, and then summer dried it out hard and flat as a manhole cover, and the dog somehow pried it up, leaving only beaver oil on the road, and *ate it*. Sure, he barfed later. Wouldn't you?

Two: Young sparrow. I kid you not. Sparrow falls from nest in the pine by the fence, flutters down ungainly to unmerciful earth, dog leaps off porch like large hairy mutant arrow, gawps bird in half an instant. Man on porch roars *drop it!* Dog emits bird with a choking coughing sound, as if disgusted by a misplaced apostrophe. Bird staggers for a moment and then flutters awkwardly up to fence post. I wouldn't have believed this if I had not seen it with my own holy eyeballs. Wonder how fledgling bird explained *that* adventure to mom.

Three: Crayons. I don't even want to think about this ever again. Crayola. The big box—sixty-four crayons, all colors. Sure, he barfed later. Sure he did. Wouldn't you?

Four: Yellow jackets. Every summer. Even though he gets stung again and again in the nether reaches of his mouth and throat, and jumps up whirling around in such a manner that we laugh so hard we have to pee. He cannot resist snapping them out of the air as if they were bright bits of candy, and then whirling around making high plaintive sounds like a country singer on laughing gas. I have to pee.

Five: Jellyfish on the shore of the vast and unpacific Pacific. Why would you ever do such a thing? What could possibly look less appetizing than an oozing quivering deceased jellyfish? Yet he does. Sure, he barfs.

Six through nineteen (some nonorganic highlights): Pencil nubs. Lacrosse balls. The cricket ball a friend sent me from Australia. Pennies. Postcards. Sports sections. Bathrobe belts. Kindling. Kazoos. Most of a paperback copy of *Harry Potter and the Order of the Phoenix*. Most of a cell-phone charger. Pen caps. Toothbrushes. One of two tiny sneakers that belonged to a child one month old, although to be fair it wasn't like the kid was actually *using* the sneakers, so why all the yelling? Was that called for? I think not.

Twenty: An entire red squirrel, called a chickaree here. *I* think the squirrel was suicidal. If *you* were a squirrel the size of a banana, and *you* could evade a dog with the athletic gifts and predatory instinct of Michael Jordan, would *you* venture down to the grass for any reason whatsoever, knowing that the dog could change you from present to past tense in less than a second? Would you? Me neither. But the squirrel did. The skull appeared magically in the grass two days later. There are so many more things that the dog ate that to fixate on, say, the back half of the squirrel is to miss the admirable *bravura* of his appetite. Still— that was a *huge* squirrel, and even half was a serious amount of meat. Sure, he barfed, but that was in the neighbor's yard. ◆

What Fathers Say, What Daughters Hear

CHARLES RAFFERTY

Just have one.
The world will come to an end before bedtime, and anyone who leaves cookies in the jar is a sucker.

I love you.
But not as much as your sister.

Daddy doesn't have time for that right now.
Daddy just poured a fresh glass of wine.

Don't get into cars with strangers.
You need to learn more about strangers!

Is your homework done?
Your mother and I hate you.

You can't go to the party until your room is cleaned.
You need to shove all these books and clothes and dirty plates into random drawers.

Take out the trash.
Pick up dog shit with your bare hands and wipe it on your pillow.

Who wants to earn an allowance?
Who wants to be owned?

I think we should buy a kitten today!
Daddy will tell you some terrible news before the end of the weekend.

Let's not ask Mommy any more questions tonight.
Mommy forgot to fill her prescription and the pharmacy is closed.

It's time to get up.
It's time to play "Don't Get Yelled At by Daddy."

I want the best for you.
Your happiness means nothing to me.

When you get to be my age, you'll understand.
When you're my age, the brainwashing will be complete.

Will his parents be home?
Are you trying to plan an orgy?

He seems like a nice boy.
I hear he's impotent.

I don't like the way women are portrayed in this movie.
Women who act like this will have their pick of the boys.

I'll be back in twenty minutes.
You won't have enough time to invite someone over to have sex.

Stop fighting with your sister.
Slam the door in my face and listen to music at full volume.

No more TV for a week!
No more TV until I leave for work or take a shower.

Do you want to hear about when your mother and I first kissed?
Do you want to throw up?

How many times do I have to tell you this?
I love hearing the sound of my angry, disappointed voice.

I'm going to build a bonfire in the backyard.
I'm going to create a smokescreen to mask the scent of the cigarette I'll be having behind the shed.

Can you do a load of laundry for me?
Can you leave a pile of my work clothes to mildew inside the washing machine all weekend?

After this show, it's time for bed.
After this show, it's time for bed. Then your mother and I will stay up drinking wine, and if you're still awake, you'll spend the next half hour hugging the pillow around your ears.

That's a nice dress.
That covers you up enough that I forget you're a girl.

Mommy and Daddy are going out to dinner tonight, so we'll need you to be on your best behavior while we're gone.
One of you will have to act as lookout. Otherwise, you're sure to be caught. ◆

When the GOP Takes Away My Birth Control, How Will I Know What Day It Is?

CAITLIN BRADY

As a woman already struggling to figure out how my body works and what to do with it, hence my need to consult conservative, white, mostly elderly men and their reproductive legislation, I'm very upset that these same people, my mental shepherds and moral guardians, are taking away my pocket calendar. Gentlemen, if I can't comprehend and make decisions about my body, how do you expect me to grasp a concept as complex as time, especially time broken down into units? That's crazy.

Yes, I have a phone. But what if its battery dies? Yes, I have a wristwatch, too—but I can't read it. It's just for style, and it doesn't even have numbers on it. What if there's one of these electromagnetic pulses you all talk so much about, and obese Chinese hackers bring down the grid? Donald Trump has said it himself—you can only trust messages rendered on good old-fashioned paper. Following this logic, I purchased a wall calendar, but it took me two months to realize I'd hung it upside down. I thought all the horses were supposed to be on their backs, falling into the sky. And honestly, you can't expect me to handle all those boxes. It's too many boxes for me, a woman.

Unless I have a hormonal pill, which I ceremoniously consume once each day while looking at the day of the week printed as a tiny purple abbreviation, I swear to you on the holiest of books, I cannot tell what day it is. The only way I can understand time, and thus the universe, is through my menstrual cycle, because, once more, I'm a woman. Menstruating and procreating are critical to my identity not just within this society and country, but also to my existence in the third dimension, as well as the so-called fourth dimension, in which time is regarded as analogous to linear dimensions. If I don't know when my period is—you guessed it—I not only bleed at random, but also cease to physically exist. I know arbitrary bleeding from the vagina upsets my mental shepherds, moral guardians, and sexual keepers, but the way my vision fades into white fuzz and I lose sensation in my limbs before floating upward, dissipating into a vapor, makes me feel not only farther away from you, but also from my own purity.

Without my tiny pill calendar, I dissolve into an unknown and unknowably dark space devoid of biological identity. It's terrifying! There's no gravity. No light. No sound. No heat. I'm afraid that the amorphous particulate cloud I become could at any time encounter alien life-forms that commune with or value me in something other than a sexual context. Would you ever wish that upon me?

Perhaps a final reason I require a hormonal pill each day to tell time, other than because time and my biology are intrinsically linked, is that I will have no other means of informing you, my mental shepherds, moral guardians, sexual keepers, and hot cum-squirting stallions, of my sexual availability. We know that when I'm sexually unavailable it's a big old pain, and nothing upsets me more than upsetting you. But with hormonal birth control to tell time, I can correlate days of the week, and month, to an appetizing array of physical symptoms, including acne, breast pain, overeating, constipation, dizziness, and vomiting—harbingers of when the glorious hour of our physical union is nigh.

In conclusion, please, please mental shepherds, moral guardians, sexual keepers, hot cum-squirting stallions, and interdimensional gender-definition warriors, don't take away my most reliable means of telling time. While I need men to tell me what's best for my body, you can't always be available when I struggle with the days of the week. Even in the catastrophic event of an EMP, or another act of unprecedented global cyber-terror, my pill packet will continue to reliably help me tell time, as well as my sexual availability for you—but most critically, it will prevent my body from dissolving into another dimension, one in which I'm not a woman at all. ◆

The Insomniac's To-Do List

JODY MACE

A Guide to Getting Things Done at 3 a.m.

1. Keep close track of exactly how much sleep you'd get if you fell asleep right now. Repeat every half hour.

2. Ponder why you said the dumbass thing you said today. If you didn't say a dumbass thing today, revisit one you said sixteen years ago, at a job you used to have, to people you don't know anymore. Consider how badly those people must think of you.

3. Resolve to use this time wisely. Think about cleaning the bathroom but then, instead, decide to do some serious writing, unlike the stupid writing you do for a living.

4. Berate yourself for doing stupid writing for a living. Imagine the disgust that both the seventeen-year-old you and your high school English teacher would feel for you if they knew the kind of writing you'd end up doing.

5. Wonder if your high school English teacher would remember you, despite the brilliance you demonstrated when you wrote that farce about archetypes. Consider the notion that perhaps you never were brilliant, but really just a smart-ass.

6. Wonder what the fuck that noise was.

7. Entertain an extremely disturbing thought: How many insects are in this house right at this very moment?

8. Become convinced that there is a microscopic bug crawling on your leg. Challenge yourself to not scratch. Dammit.

9. Remember about bedbugs. Google how to check for bedbugs. Feel sick. Seriously disgusted.

10. Read a book.

11. Realize that you've lost your attention span for reading. Or maybe it's your rapidly worsening short vision that's the problem. In either case, consider that it may be caused by a brain tumor.

12. Google brain tumors and learn that you definitely have one.

13. Think about making a video for your children with all the advice you'd like to leave them, like how to choose a mate and how to set goals. Then remember that they don't listen to you anyway, so fuck it.

14. Instead, plan the music you'd like at your funeral. Start a "Funeral Playlist" on Spotify. Include some Morrissey because every funeral should have some Morrissey songs.

15. Make a list of all the things you've been neglecting to do. Make sure to include the oil change that your car is 1,560 miles overdue for, and your mammogram.

16. Panic.

17. Find a bottle of expired Ativan and wonder if expired Ativan will just not work, or if it will harm you.

18. Think about your teenagers and compile a list of all the things that worry you about them. Start with your older one, who's in college. Is she eating enough? Does your younger one spend too much time playing video games and watching *Dr. Who* reruns?

19. Move onto things that they don't do but *might do someday*, like binge drink, drive recklessly, and smoke crack. If people still smoke crack. Research what the popular drugs are with the kids these days. Feel nostalgic about pot.

20. Consider what the chances are that, in your forties, you'll actually lose weight and decide that all your exercising has been a waste of time. Think of other people in their forties who are skinny and hate them. I mean, seriously, seriously hate them because they eat whatever they want and don't exercise—and look at them. Assholes.

21. Read an article about how lack of sleep can make you gain weight and can also adversely affect your mental health. Freak out about how you will never sleep again and you'll end up the size of a house and also

deranged and when you die they'll have to take the door off its hinges to carry you out, and they'll put you in a double-size coffin and that's all anybody will think about at the funeral, not the playlist you put together for their enjoyment.

22. Calculate the very latest you can wake up and still get your son to school on time. Set your alarm.

23. Don't think. Don't think. Don't think. ◆

Transition Brief

B . A . E A S T

Good morning and thank you for coming. Let me begin with a clear statement of what we do and why we do it. Our objectives are clear because they have to be, and to achieve this clarity we did many things. We went around in circles looking at our objectives and we came to one conclusion: Someone had to do something.

To get started we developed partnerships aimed at strategizing the planning process for next steps, with a view toward implementing best practices that address shared interests and common values going forward into the future. By leveraging synergies and synchronizing strategies we de-conflicted incompatibilities to craft a joint policy outlining five key pillars, which you already know.

We have a saying in government and it goes like this: "We've got to be able to walk and chew gum at the same time. "And we've got to work on working on that, too.

Our efforts fit into three broad categories, which are program development, program implementation, and program evaluation. All of which feed the beginning of the cycle, which is the funding request.

On program development, we are engaged in an optimization process that builds partner capacity, and the first question we ask in addressing capacity is, "Where do we begin?" And it's been agreed: We've got to begin somewhere.

If we look back five years we know we couldn't have predicted all the events that occurred to put us here, in the present, today, so it's entirely unnecessary of me to say that looking ahead five years will not allow us to predict the factors that will contribute to future threats, which are evolving. We must remain flexible but resilient as we develop stakeholder plans that are as wide-reaching as they are focused. Because at the end of the day, it's a multiyear process requiring strategic patience and sustainability.

I'd like to add one sort of subnote here, which is to say that it's important to balance the needs of our communities with an overarching structure that nests our specific objectives in a larger context. Doing so creates the possibility of disengaging from our initial design plan, whether as a permanent off-ramp or as a transition to the next activity.

Because, whatever it is, we don't want to be doing this forever.

Turning to implementation, we do many different things, and I'm happy to go into detail, but I want to focus on three, which I'm sure you've already heard. We looked at the different drivers and how they manifested themselves, which allowed us to focus on one issue, to great effect, which I'll go into later. But here are just a few, and the laundry list is long:

- Democracy
- Prosperity
- Corruption
- The environment
- Education, and
- Everything else

Take a corollary issue: the insidious nature of global jihadi networks that prevent quality education for the girl-child in creating broader economic inclusivity for disenfranchised populations all over the world everywhere. Whether you know it or not, these challenges occur on a daily, weekly, and monthly basis. I mean, we ask ourselves, "How in the world are we to know how to address the individual needs of each community all the time?"

And the answer is, "Yes."

Third: Metrics. Our work is all about metrics, which are all about coordination, with all the relevant parts of government working together to vie for a piece of the pie, which goes to the winner and proves a measure of success. There's funding but it's never enough. We have to make tough decisions and there's no silver bullet for judging progress, although in one case we evaluated ourselves against a theory of change and found ourselves to be successful. Which was pretty good.

In closing, I'll add that we must think outside the box to evolve new para-digms that address the needs of target populations, including youth, vulner-able women and children, disaffected minorities, the poor, the uneducated, the homeless, the aimless, the hapless, and the deprived.

People.

It may be a catchphrase in government to say that if we do this right, we'll work ourselves out of a job. But I'm not worried about that.

So thank you for coming. I'm sorry to leave so soon. Please stay in touch so that you can receive us when transition occurs again. ◆

Stand-Up Comedian

BRIAN BEDARD

Until the morning we found the mouse lying dead on the produce room floor, I actually envied it. It lived a daring life, dwelling in the basement of that decrepit old building among the cobwebs and headless mannequins, the bent milk crates and rusted barber chairs (the building had housed more businesses than I can name), hiding in the basement during the day and raiding the produce department by night. I thought of the mouse as a kind of rodent Zorro, who, though it had no sword, needed no sword. It left its mark with razor-sharp teeth on ears of corn, stalks of celery, and large button mushrooms. Little zigzags. Circles. McDonald's arches. (Did the mouse wear yellow tights and a red cape?) It left a kind of terrorist graffiti, and this really irked the produce manager, Scoop, a World War II veteran of the Pacific Campaign, who walked with a limp and had an obsession with pineapple displays.

The mouse had nerve, speed, agility, and good taste. It always picked the best ears of corn, the nicest mushrooms and, with an almost perverse relish, it took just enough bites of the choicest items so that we'd have to throw them all away. What's more, the mouse had been doing this for most of the winter and into the spring, showing itself only on rare occasions. By June, though, it was getting bolder, or lazy, or both. A jaded criminal drunk on its own success.

Several mornings a week the mouse would still be nibbling away on a head of Chinese cabbage when Scoop would yank the black plastic tarp off the vegetable rack, and Larry, poised for action by the tomato display, would let fly with a small rutabaga or potato, banging it off the mirror above the mouse's head. And away the mouse would go, streaking down the back of the rack, dodging more potatoes, Brussels sprouts, Italian prunes, and disappearing in the wall somewhere. It was great fun watching Scoop jerk the tarp back like a magician and then see the vegetable rack suddenly turn into a carnival arcade with a live target leaping and weaving as the artillery bounced off the mirrors. I tried a few throws myself from time to time, using shriveled lemons or limes, but the mouse was not to be taken out that way.

We were all surprised to find it dead one Monday morning on the floor in the back room, curled slightly in an attitude of supplication and hardened into that pose by rigor mortis. Somewhere, somehow, in the network of its quick little mouse brain it had short-circuited, grown lazy, maybe bored with the regular cuisine and, like us humans, gambling against its best instincts, sampled the d-Con that Scoop had thrown in frustration into a corner behind a pallet covered with sacks of onions. What greater illusion of immortality than a run of sweet luck?

I don't remember whose idea it was to put a mushroom in the mouse's front paws and stand it on the trimming table below the row of knives we kept in a rack on the wall, but once we set the mouse in position with a lettuce leaf prop to assure its balance, it looked great. We all waited for Billy Joe Wendt, our high school dropout night shift kid, who sometimes helped us on Monday morning and who spent most of his waking hours stoned, to show up. (His standard question after punching in and putting on his apron was to turn to Scoop and ask, "When can I go home?") That morning, though, he didn't ask when he could go home. He spotted the mouse standing on the trimming table, smiled the most delighted smile I'd seen him produce in the year I'd known him, and said, "How did you get him to stand up?" ◆

Keep Calm and Kill These Mimes

ALLISON K. WILLIAMS

It's been a long two weeks stage-managing a street festival in Macedonia.

I'm looking up the night bus to Thessaloniki. Pane, my boss, looks over.

"Don't take the bus. It's not comfortable for you."

I say, "The bus is fine."

Pane says, "Bus takes five hours from 2 a.m. Take my car."

I am skeptical. Pane, civic leader/mafia don of Skopje, offers nothing without a price.

"Take my car to Strumitsa, catch the bus there. Thessaloniki only thirty minutes," Pane says. "You take my guys to Strumitsa on the way."

There's the price.

"Gig tonight, big dance club, very popular. You hang out, you dance, tomorrow morning easy bus to Thessaloniki."

"Why don't you just give them the car?"

Pane rolls his eyes. "You drive my guys, OK?"

I take the keys.

Two guys in whiteface, striped T-shirts, black pants, and red suspenders walk over. Mimes.

Pane says, "Vojo, Zlatko. Allison gonna drive you, you bring it back."

They nod and smile. Silently. They tell me—in mime—they're happy to meet me, let's go!

Vojo and Zlatko pile in. A smell permeates the car and I get why Pane wants me to drive. Skopsko. The most popular beer in Macedonia. The festival's big sponsor. Evidently, the mimes have been paid in beer.

On the highway, I hear a carbonated hiss and check the mirror. Vojo and Zlatko have opened a big bottle of Skopsko. They pour themselves generous cups and offer one to me.

"Ahhh, no thanks—do you have open container laws here?"

They mime puzzlement, bewilderment, confusion. I slow down to avoid any curious police.

Vojo points to the speedometer, tapping an imaginary watch. They act out wind whooshing their hair. I ignore them.

Two hours later it's black post-Communist countryside night. I've seen plenty of signs—all in Cyrillic. Vojo points urgently to a gas station. I pull over, hoping the clerk speaks drunk mime.

They get back in the car. I pull back on the road. "OK, where?"

The mimes throw up their arms and widen their eyes.

"Didn't you get directions?"

Vojo holds up a plastic bag. They bought more cups.

"Guys. Are we even near Strumitsa?"

Zlatko nods.

"OK, how close?"

Zlatko does something poetic with five fingers.

"Five minutes? Five kilometers? Five days? I get it, you're mimes! Now you're lost mimes! Two people here speak Macedonian when they want to, so one of them should get directions!"

Vojo and Zlatko exchange glances and mime a volcano erupting from someone's head. They rock imaginary babies and pat air-kittens.

I am not calmed. I want to kill them.

I slam on the brakes next to a startled pedestrian. "Ask him where the club is!"

The mimes squeeze together out the window. The pedestrian gawks at our clown car. From the waist up, Vojo and Zlatko dance. They do the sprinkler. They raise the roof.

Light dawns in the pedestrian's face. "Select!" He jabbers positively in Macedonian.

The mimes give him imaginary thank-you presents and slide back in. They make steering wheels—turn left here! Go straight!

We park behind an industrial building pulsing with music. Inside, the crowd is the usual Eastern European mix—supermodel-quality girls and hairy, troll-shaped guys, spandex minidresses and hot-pink tank tops blazoned with silver sequins.

I'm not sure "mime" fits this demographic.

The music changes and Vojo and Zlatko emerge onto a small stage. They begin a classic, Marcel Marceau-style mime act. And then—in a country where 40 percent of the population still believes "being gay is a crime that warrants jail"—they play a love scene. Zlatko gives Vojo a flower. They look bashfully at each other, then look away while their hands find each other and hold on. Vojo proposes on one knee, Zlatko joyfully accepts.

It.

Kills.

The crowd stays rapt throughout the entire two-mimes-in-a-dance-club situation, and roars approval.

I catnap in the dressing room through two more sets, cheers filtering through my sleep-haze.

I wake to Vojo wiping makeup off and barefaced Zlatko packing half-full Skopsko bottles.

Vojo speaks. "Good sleep?"

I nod.

"OK, give me keys. Bus station is right, that way three blocks, left. Big square."

I nod.

They give me beery hugs and air-kisses. They chorus, *"Doviduvanje!"*

I probably won't see them later. But I step back and gesture—to my heart, then toward Vojo and Zlatko, encircling empty air. Their laughter floats down with me to the street, where the sun is rising, where I follow their good directions. ◆

Hardware

CHRIS OFFUTT

During my freshman year of college I worked part-time at a hardware store, a job for which I was ill-suited, considering how little I knew about hardware. When customers asked for a particular item, I led them to the appropriate aisle and pretended to seek what they wanted, while hoping they'd spot it themselves. The boss was kind, an older man who took a paternal interest in me. Despite my colossal ignorance, he didn't want to fire me. Instead, he found me a job he hoped I could handle.

He assigned me to assemble bicycles in the storeroom, but I could never get the hand brakes to work properly. Next, he put me in charge of delivering large objects such as grills and lawnmowers. The delivery truck was old, with a rusty manual stick shift that came out of the floorboards. I couldn't maneuver it past first gear, which made for very long trips—too long from the boss's perspective—and he decided that I should make copies of keys in a miniature vice. The keys I produced were ragged slivers of very thin metal that wouldn't fit any lock in existence. More than once I ground the blank key into a stub. Mainly I excelled at filling the air with metal dust.

Because the boss liked me, the assistant manager didn't. He referred to my severe acne as "jack bumps," explaining that they were the result of excessive masturbation. I didn't say anything, wondering what counted as excessive, or even moderate. I was eighteen.

One slow afternoon the assistant manager sent me to the backroom to find a board-stretcher. I looked and looked without success. Then he tasked me with going to another hardware store, our crosstown rival, to buy one there. The clerk at that store sent me to a sawmill at the edge of town. The sawmill manager told me he'd just gotten rid of his last one but he'd heard a guy up Lick Fork Holler had a used one for sale. Determined to prove my worth, I drove up the dirt road that flanked Lick Fork Creek.

A fierce-looking man stood in the front yard wearing overalls and boots with no shirt. Six or so dogs milled about, barking at my presence. I rolled the window down and yelled that I'd heard he had a used board-stretcher for sale. He asked me to repeat myself and I did. He then took a few steps toward the truck and asked again. I told him and he moved closer, and again wanted to know what I was saying. I figured he was hard of hearing and began yelling to him. In this fashion, he eventually crossed his entire yard to my car, the dogs still barking and swarming around his boots. He turned out to be a very big man with a ferocious face—scarred and marred and pocked like his head had caught on fire and someone tried to put it out with an ice pick.

He explained to me that there was no such thing as a board-stretcher. He suggested that someone was pranking with me. I didn't have the heart to tell him that it wasn't a single person, but an entire network of people enjoying themselves at my expense. I thanked him and prepared to leave.

"Is that acne on your face?" he said. "Them dots and all."

"Yes," I said.

"They done me the same way," he said. "When I was thirty-five years old, it went away and ain't never come back. You'll be all right. Just got to wait it out."

I drove away, terrified that I still had seventeen years to go, that I might wind up looking like him. As it turned out, I was ahead of the game. My acne went away at age thirty, the year I got married. I suppose they were jack bumps after all. ◆

Bride of Christ

LORRI MCDOLE

My sister, the nun, is getting married.

OK, she's not really a nun—she'd rather be anything (dead, for example) than Catholic—but for years now Jesus has been the only guy good enough for her. And if not having sex for forty years and counting doesn't make you a nun, it does make you a minority, sometimes even a commodity.

Wendy *has* dated, over the years. The last guy (four years ago?) was Matt, a nice-looking man she met at the Calvary Temple church she attends three times a week. She liked him well enough until she discovered that his career with the liquor control board was just fancy talk for slinging booze at the local liquor store. In my sister's Pentecostal religion (the one we both grew up with), abstinence applies to a lot more than just plain old sex. Even if the mouths of those shiny bottles never touched Matt's lips, Wendy couldn't stand the idea of his hands all over them. I still remember the look on her face when my ten-year-old daughter (her niece!) showed her our new china cabinet. "And this," Carson said, sweeping her arm proudly, "is where we keep our margarita glasses!" As if she, too, were in the habit of knocking back a few with the neighbors on weekends.

Three years before that, Wendy dated another guy from church, Randy, who turned out to have a problem with (you guessed it, love those affliction-appropriate names!) porn. Jesus may have been all about the sinners, but Wendy didn't think He wanted her to date one of them. I have to admit it kind of creeped me out when she told me. I remembered Randy helping me with a golf swing in my backyard, and just thinking about him putting his hands on *me* after touching all those sticky pictures, that sticky keyboard, that sticky . . . stick . . .

Years before *that* there was the handsome medical student, Tom, who was prone to accidents (the kind where only other people get hurt), and Wes, who chased Wendy for six years only to get engaged to another woman right before Wendy figured out that God was trying to tell her that he was "the one."

When this new guy, Len, told Wendy after they had dated a mere two months that God was telling *him* that *she* was the one—well, you can see why she jumped at this latter-day chance to obey, even though everyone knows that God is as patient as death.

My family has mixed emotions about this engagement, which happened, as things do, just when we'd given up on it for good. My mother the hypochondriac is happy to see Wendy settled before she dies from diabetes (or tachycardia, or an enlarged liver, or that funny pain in her leg, but not, she's quick to point out, from the millions of cigarettes she's smoked over the last fifty years), but is worried she'll have to wear something other than a muumuu to the wedding. My father, who received a divorce from my mother thirty years ago and never had the courage to remarry, counts on Wendy's sympathetic ear for hours a week and is surely hearing the words of *his* father right about now. "Just wait," Grandpa Jim used to say. "One day your daughters will get married and break your heart, just like mine did me." (I'm not sure Dad's heart even cracked when I got married fourteen years ago, but then I did leave him Wendy, sacrificing the virgin.)

When my brother, who's just cycled out of Western State Hospital and is still basking in the lucidity of lithium, heard the news, all he had to say was, "It's about *fuckin'* time; what is she, forty-*fuckin'*-one?" Amen, brother.

As for me, the "forty-year-old virgin for a sister" shtick will be hard to give up. But hey, I'm family, in it for the long haul. Besides, Len the fiancé is a pastor. And considering that Wendy received her first kiss at age fourteen from the married pastor of our Assemblies of God church (who so surprised her at the altar when she thought she was alone that his big pillow lips fit entirely inside the oval of her gasping mouth), I don't care if my sister *is* forty-fuckin'-one—for my money, this story's just getting good. ◆

Throw Them Off the Train

DENIS HORGAN

It was a test; any dope could see that. They were playing me for a fool, seeing how much they could get away with from the new baby-faced editor and publisher of the *Bangkok World* newspaper—namely, me. Through astonishing-to-this-day happenstances, I was the *bossissimo* of the paper after several undistinguished years as a US Army officer, helping to lose the grand wars raging through Southeast Asia in those distant days just before the Disco Era. I had been warned of the malevolent dealings of the crowd over at the *Bangkok Post*, so it was no surprise when our Thai general manager stopped me in the hall and gravely informed me that they were once more throwing our papers off the train.

"This for us is not so very good," he said in his uneven English—an English still leagues better than my Thai.

Not good? We only sold a few thousand copies at the US air bases up-country, but a few thousand was a lot for our newspaper, whose circulation was around thirteen thousand—give or take five thousand or so.

This had happened before. The sly *Bangkok Post* crew had already found a way to kick our bundles off the early morning train. I had sent them a brisk message of complaint and heard back in the most oleaginous terms how they were astonished and amazed that such a thing could happen, and they would rather have the nails pulled from their fingers than be in any way part of such a shoddy practice, and wasn't it only just another sad sign of the contentious and troubling times we live in, giving a bad name to all good professionals and institutions—although surely not your respectful friends and admirers over here at the *Bangkok Post*—and we hope you are having a very nice day.

Not buying that for a second I had sternly advised my people, "Throw *their* papers off the train." The rural landscape would then be littered with *Bangkok Posts* and *Bangkok Worlds* until the game grew wearying and petered out.

"They have a spy in our business office who's telling them when to hurt us the most," Giorgio Berlingieri, one of our owners, said with an operatic arch of his eyebrows and a conductor's wave of the hands at the great perfidy of it all, the dark debasement of all that is good and noble.

"That's terrible," I said. "How do we know they have a spy in our office?"

"Because my spy in their office told me," he replied.

Then I learned that *Post* agents were once again jettisoning our lovely newspapers. In high exasperation and even higher dudgeon, with as much steel as I could muster, I commanded my employees to retaliate: "Throw them off the train."

It hardly seems fair that I should be faulted for every minor thing that goes astray when conflicting appreciations of richly various languages scratch up against one another. Who could ever believe that a gentle, poetical sort such as your pal, Denis Horgan, Editor and Publisher of the *Bangkok World*, would think for even an instant that the "them" in "Throw them off the train" would be construed to mean not bundles of newspapers, but, alas, the agents of the *Bangkok Post*? Yet those worthy gentlemen were indeed hurled from the train into rural rice paddies by our own men.

Of course, there being so little understanding of life's little mishaps, a great howl went up from the *Bangkok Post*, assailing me to all ears as a criminal madman for inflicting such an outrage, though you'd expect just that from a misplaced cowboy, some crude American gangster cousin of Mr. Al Capone of Chicago, USA, pickled in violence and twisted in disproportion and . . .

. . . and never again did a single copy of the *Bangkok World* get tossed from the early morning train en route to Vientiane across the Mekong, with connections to Korat and Ubon and Udorn and other such exotic places, and never again did farmers along the route sleep anything but the sleep of babes, knowing they were free of the rain of falling newspapers and flailing enemy agents. ◆

Writing Advice to My Students that Would Also Have Been Good Sex Advice for My High-School Boyfriends

HELENA DE BRES

- Assume your audience is skeptical and easily bored.

- Avoid making bold assertions you're unprepared to back up.

- It's generally better to delve deeply into one or two areas than to spread yourself thinly over five.

- If you're stuck, organize the body into sections and work on different sections at different times.

- Slow down.

- Make clear what you mean by any unusual terms you introduce.

- Irrelevant digressions disrupt the flow and are confusing.

- A large part of the skill here lies in knowing what to put in and what to leave out.

- Don't make your audience do all the work in figuring out how the various parts fit together.

- Ask yourself: "Do I really want to put this here, or would it make more sense somewhere else?"

- Be sure to anticipate and respond to objections to your position.

- If you think you absolutely need to quote an author, do so sparingly.

- Don't introduce sudden surprises in the conclusion.

- If complications arise, meet with me well before the due date. ◆

Intro to Creative Writing

DANI JOHANNESEN

Professor Stevens dislikes donuts; the icing gets stuck in his beard. Fridays he breakfasts at Burger King before heading out to the lake, where he smokes cigarettes on the shore and ignores his wife's phone calls. He idolizes James Dickey. He's no good at fiction. The department chair's out to get him.

He strolls into his classroom wearing his uniform—faded black jeans that sag in the rear and a worn fleece pullover. He slings his bag onto the table up front and checks his watch—he's five minutes late, as usual. The students are already seated, and he surveys the assembly. In the back row a girl scribbles furiously in a fancy journal. Against the far wall a young man in sweat pants and a Minnesota Twins hat snores quietly—his desk empty, except for his head. In the front row Stevens spots Dana, the notorious overachiever, pretending to read *Finnegans Wake*.

Plastering on a smile, he welcomes the students to Intro to Creative Writing and orders them to take out a pencil and notebook. The kid in the Twins hat scrambles to borrow a pen from the girl sitting next to him.

"Write down the name of your favorite poet and five things you know something about," Stevens commands. "You have five minutes."

He watches the assortment of faces—some intently focused on their lists, others panicked, staring at blank sheets of paper. A girl near the door smacks her gum and gazes up at the clock.

After five minutes, he asks for volunteers to share their lists. Dana's hand shoots up. She's happy to be there.

"My favorite poet is T. S. Eliot," she says. "He's so wonderfully complicated."

Stevens scowls and shakes his head, stuffs his hands in his pockets, and mutters something under his breath about the "catastrophe of modernism" before turning toward the chalkboard. He digs a piece of yellow chalk from his bag and scrawls on the board: WRITE WHAT YOU KNOW. He knows Sioux City, Iowa. Pole-vaulting. Cattle and blonde bank tellers. Another hand emerges.

"Professor Stevens, uh, I grew up on a farm. No one wants to read about that. My hero is Hunter S. Thompson."

Stevens spots the voice's owner—a skinny young man in a Bob Dylan T-shirt, skintight jeans, and checkerboard-pattern Vans sneakers. Stevens looks down at his class roster.

"Bobby Jorgenson?"

"Yeah."

"You grew up on a farm?"

"Yeah. Over by Bowdle. *Fear and Loathing* changed my life."

"Uh huh. Have you ever dropped acid, Bobby?"

"Uh, no."

"Ever been on a road trip?"

"Uh, just to Rapid City."

"Any plans to one day have your cremated ashes shot from a canon?"

"Huh. Uh, hadn't really thought about it. That'd be pretty sweet though."

The kid in the Twins hat smiles and nods at Bobby approvingly.

"What else is on your list, Bobby?"

"OK, so, for stuff I know something about I put 'post-modernism,' 'Family Guy,' I'm taking a class in logic so I put 'deductive reasoning,' uh, 'poetry,' and 'asstetics.'"

"What was that last one?"

"Asstetics. You know, beauty and stuff."

Dumbfounded but hardly surprised, Stevens shuffles back to the table in front of the room, noisily pulls the chair out, and plops down into it. He stares out the window that faces the street; it's a still December night—no traffic, no sirens, no obnoxious noise or light. Across the street, a string of colored Christmas lights wrapped around a porch railing glow beneath a blanket of thick snow. He'd rather be on the can reading Richard Wilbur. He turns back to the class.

"Your first assignment is to write a poem about corn."

The girl in the back looks up from her journal. Bobby furrows his eyebrows. The kid in the Twins hat quickly writes down the assignment, CORN, at the top of his single sheet of paper.

Dana's hand shoots up.

"But Professor Stevens, I want to write complicated poems."

Stevens picks up his chalk and turns back to the board: CORN IS COMPLICATED.

"You can go ahead and get started." ◆

On My Head

THADDEUS RUTKOWSKI

My first haircut was a flattop. I got it below street level, in a decrepit barber-shop my father took me to. Outside, there was a kinetic red-and-white signpost. Inside, there were cast-iron chairs with leather strops hanging from their sides. The whole place smelled like scalps.

The barber used electric clippers on my head. Behind my ears, the clippers made my entire skull vibrate. Then the barber applied paste that made my head look like a bur.

I used a comb on my head, along with a large dose of goop. When I was finished, my head looked like a skillet.

Later, my mother gave me a trim. When she was finished, I looked like I was wearing a helmet that had failed to stop a grazing bullet.

For a long while I stayed away from barbers of all stripes. My hair grew until it reached my back.

One day I saw some boys with Mohawk cuts. But these boys weren't Mohawks; they weren't even Native Americans. They were just a couple of white boys trying to look like Native Americans. Even so, I decided to get a brush of my own.

One night I went into a convenience store, and the cashier asked me, "What are you?"

"I'm a boy," I said, "I guess."

"Seriously," the cashier said, "I can't tell."

Another time, at a border between countries, a guard looked at my passport and asked, "Who is this? Is this a little girl?"

"It is not time for jokes," I said in the guard's language.

"For me," the guard said in my language, "it is always time for jokes."

On another occasion, I walked through an airport and was stopped by two plainclothesmen. "Do you take acid?" they asked. "You look like you do."

Later, a girlfriend talked me into getting a layered style and a body wave. After I got them, she said, "You look so good I want to have sex with you right now."

Later still, I was invited to a "clipping party," where men with short hair were getting their hair cut even shorter by a barber wearing Army fatigues. The sergeant/barber buzzed the clipees' heads with electric shears. A man with a razor hanging from his belt stood nearby. He said his name was Bic. I flipped through a scrapbook of boot camp photographs, but I didn't sign up for a haircut.

One time, I met a performer whose hair was shaped like a cylinder. The cylinder was about twelve inches high. I spoke to him, but our conversation had nothing to do with appearance. The next time we met, the cylinder was gone and he was wearing a hair net.

These days I go to a cutter who has hair that resembles my own. When he asks me what I want, I say, "I want my hair short in places but long in others. I want it long enough for a ponytail, but I also want to see bare scalp. I want words scored in the stubble. I want to wear ceremonial hair gear. I want to be stopped by cops. I want to be on television. I want groupies. I want a style among the top one hundred. I want to meet relatives. I want to be photographed with family." ◆

Prayer for a Friend Who Has Deactivated Her Facebook Account

WENDY BRENNER

O God, whose merciful wisdom reaches to the uttermost parts of creation, including social media, please watch over and guide our friend Haley who as of last night or very early this morning deactivated her Facebook account and none of us know why. Assist us, O Lord, as we seek to understand the reason for Haley's vanishment from our News Feeds, and strengthen us so that we might bear the burden of grief, worry, and confusion her absence inflicts upon us, even though we haven't actually seen or spoken to Haley since our senior year in high school during which she always had a smile on her face (though who knows what she was smoking in the parking lot every morning, our own recollections of those mornings being somewhat vague). Perhaps Haley's cheerfulness was a brave front even then, Lord, to cover up deep-seated psychological problems that might explain why now she would just suddenly and rudely abandon her eight hundred and fifty-one Facebook friends with no explanation whatsoever. Please help us to support and comfort Haley, O heavenly Father, if she deactivated her Facebook account because she's suffering from a life-threatening illness or injury from a car wreck that was totally not her fault (like what happened to us last year with that school bus), or if she's in the midst of a breakup with her fiancé Chad whom we have never met personally but who looks like a nice guy—except for his weird plump lips, which appear to be cosmetically enhanced—in Haley's thousands of Facebook photos which as of this morning we can no longer see, photos she may have posted, we now imagine, because the relationship was already toast and she was trying to put a good face on things. And if by chance Haley recently learned that Chad is gay, which frankly we suspected all along based on his obviously injected lips (and also he reminded us of a guy we dated for an entire semester in college who suddenly turned gay for no reason) we ask that you please sustain Haley with your grace and steadfast reassurances, for example that gay men only date the most beautiful women, which we know is true because our ex-boyfriend told us this himself when he suddenly turned gay and dumped us after an entire semester of pretending to be perfectly happy with us. O Lord, we wonder whether Haley's cat Potemkin died; would that be enough of a tragedy to make her deactivate her Facebook account (and what kind of pretentious name is Potemkin, but then Haley always was a poseur, now that we think about it, carrying around that copy of *Being and Nothingness* our entire senior year even though it wasn't required for any class), or maybe she is being cyber-stalked by someone, such as an ex-boyfriend (probably not Chad, LOL, and anyway they were still "In a Relationship" as of last night); could that be the reason for her disappearance, or does she just suddenly think she's too good for Facebook, and, by extension, us?

O Lord, please let us know if Haley is mad at us.

Seriously, God. Is Haley mad at us?

If Haley is mad at us, O blessed God, please enlighten us as to *why*, since we have never failed to like her status updates even though we ourselves are not vegan nor do we have any interest in eating local, going green, thrifting, upcycling, repurposing, Etsy, Andy Borowitz, relief efforts in Rwanda, or any other of Haley's ridiculous liberal hobbies. Nevertheless, we frequently and generously comment on Haley's posts that we are praying for her and that it's never too late to accept Jesus as her Lord and Savior, and if she would just make straight her path, she would obtain everlasting life, like we did. So please look with favor upon us, almighty Father, since obviously if Haley is mad at us she is wrong and deserves your loving correction and swift punishment for the poor choices she has made, especially the choice to deactivate her Facebook account as if our feelings don't mean anything to her, as if our very existence doesn't even matter. ◆

How to Die Alone

SARAH EINSTEIN

Gaze at the woman sleeping next to you and ask yourself if she really loves you. Think of all of the reasons she shouldn't. Slowly get mad at her for not loving you enough. An hour before she has to get up for a double shift at the hospital, sob loudly until she wakes and then ask her how, after all you've done, she could be so cold. When she asks what you're talking about, lock yourself in the bathroom and refuse to discuss it until five minutes before she has to leave. If she really loves you, she'll be late for work. Again.

Tell the man who tells you that you're beautiful that you aren't. List the reasons: the frizziness of your hair, the length of your nose, the circles under your eyes, the middle age spread.

Carpet your living room in white, get a glass coffee table. Tell your sister/brother/best friend that you'd love to have them visit, but that they should get a sitter because your house isn't really child-friendly. When they stop visiting, complain that people with children abandon their friends and don't take their adult relationships seriously.

Tell new acquaintances about your allergy to wheat. Your recent biopsy. The death of your cat.

Join a church, even though you aren't really religious, because you read in a women's magazine that it's a good place to meet the sort of men who marry. Buy a bunch of flower-print dresses because you imagine that's what Christian women wear. Attend the Wednesday night Bible study and, when there aren't any single men, flirt with the married ones. Stop going after a few months; tell your friends it's because the people there weren't very welcoming. Start thinking of yourself as a Buddhist, though never bother to actually learn anything about Buddhism.

Go to bars full of people who are young enough to be there when you no longer are. Go often enough that the bartender knows your name and what you drink; drink a lot. Tell all the young women standing by the pool tables how badly love has treated you. Warn them against trusting anyone but then, in a show of continued hope, tell them that they are lovely. Ask them their names. When they don't answer, tell them yours. When they walk away from you to rejoin their friends, order another drink. Tell the bartender—again—how these kids have no respect any more. Ignore her when she suggests that maybe it's time to go home. Play "Desperado" on the jukebox and sing along instead.

Look in the mirror and ask yourself if you like what you see. Imagine that if you were a better person, you would be able to say "yes," and think about how this means you are not only ugly on the outside, but also on the inside, where it counts. ◆

The Top Ten Reasons It Is Awesome to Be a Tam-Bram American

RAVI SHANKAR

10. **First, TamBram is short for Tamilian-Brahmin,** an ethnic group whose mass media presence can be quickly summarized as: IT guy who disappears into a ceiling vent in a repetitive commercial; a sexless nerd who grows paralyzed around women on a popular sitcom; and the Quickie Mart owner known as Apu on the Simpsons.

9. Instead of stale labels of xenophobia, you get to experience the floral lushness of slurs: Elephant Jockey, Cow-Kisser, Buttonhead, Slurpee Jockey, Turbanator, Higger, and my personal favorite, Spice Rubber, which I was once called in front of a public library in Manassas where a group of teenagers had gathered for a photograph and into whose frame, oblivious, nose in book, I ambled, only to be warded off with, "Move, you fucking Spice Rubber!" If that elegant appellation hasn't been pitched to a condom manufacturer yet, you can have it. Consider it a freebie. We Indians do love freebies (although more the getting than the giving of them . . .).

8. At the fanciest occasions, like weddings, you get to eat delicacies with your fingers off a banana leaf. For real! *Dosas* and *vadas*, served with *sambar* and *rasam*. Hyderabad *biryani* with lemon rice seasoned with coconut peanuts, tamarind, chilies, curry leaves, dal, and fenugreek seeds. Thin crispy *papads*. You can even slurp warm sweet milky rice *payasam* with your hands.

7. Tamil Sangam literature is as old and storied as any in the world, so next time you're at the reception after some chichi literary event where inebriated famous writers are bandying around Horace and Ovid, you can come strong with Thiruvalluvar, the Indian Confucius, or Brahman poet

Mamulanar, whose descriptions of the Mauryan invasions of South India rival the Greeks. The post-colonials will tremble, the fat studies scholar will nibble a gherkin, and from that point in the evening onward, the gorgeous Scandinavian musicologist will appear to hover in your proximal orbit.

6. For what was essentially a narrowly nationalistic terrorist organization, not many such groups have cooler sounding names than the Tamil Tigers.

5. You get to be late to everything because you run on IST (Indian Stretchable Time). Those who are meeting with you will consider it a lovable zany cultural quirk to be celebrated, like with the French woman who requires a kiss on each cheek before you can meet.

4. You are provided with shiny-shirted uncles unrelated to you, and cousins who, while the adults are watching cricket upstairs, will huddle around the ping-pong table in the basement calling one another's junk "untouchables" and telling jokes like "how do you teach a blonde maths? You subtract her clothes, divide her legs, and square root her." The mechanics of dividing anyone's legs notwithstanding, you will never puzzle out why they pluralize math.

3. Better Gods? I'll see your Virgin Mary and raise you a Saraswati playing the *veena* on a lotus, a Lakshmi arrayed in finery and flanked by elephants, and a half-naked many-armed Kali carrying a sword, a trisula, a severed head, and a skull-cup to catch its blood.

2. Need fodder for therapy? Lucky you have an *amma* who wears a sari and a nose ring but acts like a Yiddish mother, ensuring that you never leave home without a jacket no matter what the temperature is outside, and you have an *appa* who is so cheap that he clips coupons from newspapers he borrows from the neighbors' driveways and dries out his paper towels on the windowsill to reuse.

1¾. If you can say the Tamil phrase for "I don't understand" (*puriyavillai*), then you can become an honorary Tamilian for a day and get into any temple or museum in South India for free. Trust me. Just walk straight into the Government Museum and if someone tries to stop you just say "*puriyavillai*" a half dozen times and shrug your shoulders. I promise they'll let you go on about your business. Especially if you follow that gesture with a hundred rupee note.

1½. Because you are not really Asian, on forms that require you to indicate your nationality, you can mark "Other," and write in "Indian Subcontinent." Having a subcontinent is badass.

1¼. Did I mention Tam-Brams really love their maths?

1. When someone mentions yoga, you can pretend like you know the guru who invented it; when someone mentions the spiciness of curry, you can get macho points just by mentioning you are from Madras. And the Kamasutra? Don't even get me started on the Kamasutra. ◆

Horror in the Okefenokee Swamp

SANDRA GAIL LAMBERT

The six hours of paddling and a chilly day in south Georgia mean the only reason I know my backside is there is because it always has been. Can you get frostbite on your butt? I decide you can't, but am imagining a hot shower as I paddle my kayak out of the swamp and up the canal to the marina. It's always a relief when my wheelchair is where I left it—standing sentinel at the boat ramp.

I wedge the kayak between the uneven cinder blocks at the bottom of the ramp. Now all I have to do is my usual roll out of the boat, scooch over the concrete, balance on all fours, rise onto my knees, and twist into the seat of my wheelchair. At least the cold means no one is hanging out by the water. Besides the way people act funny when I crawl by, an observer always makes something go awry—like losing my shoes or trapping one breast under the seat on my way up.

Before I can start my roll over the side, a ranger in an overcoat and gloves appears at the top of the ramp. He chats about the weather. He asks about my trip. How many alligators? Any otters? He lingers. Knees to chest, arms clasped around them to stop the shivering, I try to wait him out. He keeps talking. He is immune to my mental cursing. In the middle of his story about the year it snowed, I abandon modesty and make my moves. More than once, I am butt-first in his direction.

Panting and finally sitting face forward in my chair, I smile at the ranger. I'm pleased at my accomplishment. His neck and face are sweaty and red. His expression is professionally bland, but I can see the horror underneath. Eyes averted, he mutters something and rushes away, disappearing over the top of the ramp. This pisses me off. So what that I don't move the way he does. Why can't people just deal with—admire even—someone figuring out how to do whatever it is they want to do? Why doesn't he appreciate my skill, my ingenuity, my enthusiasm? And now he's left, right when I could use some help hauling the kayak up the ramp.

It isn't until I'm at my campsite, blood returning to my backside, that I feel something cold and bare. Have I mentioned that I don't use underwear while kayaking? It gets wet. It bunches. Squirming from side to side, I strip off the thread-worn, used-only-for-kayaking pants. I hold them in front of me. Except for three frayed strips of material, the seat is gone. That last trip along the concrete was too much for it. I had been left exposed. I picture my pasty-white-with-cold cheeks pointed at the ranger, with the ragged remains of the pants stretched across them and looking not unlike a balding man's bad comb-over.

To my disappointment, I can't stay mad about the guy's sweaty, abrupt departure. And I'm going to have to mentally apologize for my unwarranted and unkind thoughts. It turns out big naked butt cheeks waving around made him leave. If I'd mooned him right away, I'd be less cold now. I'm saving the pants. ◆

What Bad Owners Say at the Dog Park

LISE FUNDERBURG

1. He's friendly.
2. He never does that.
3. That's his way of playing.
4. He's still learning.
5. He's not so good on recall.
6. Watch out for his leash.
7. I've never seen him do that before.
8. That's his play growl.
9. Pookie, you've got the lady all tangled up in your leash.
10. It's better not to look him in the eye.
11. No jumping, Pookie.
12. Pookie just wants to give kisses, don't you, Pookie?
13. Pookie, no.
14. Did Pookie get mud on the lady with those big muddy paws?
15. Pookie, I said no. ◆

A Contributor's Note

MICHAEL MARTONE

Provided by the author, who gives permission for its use in the case his contest entry of 500 words or less is selected for reprinting in a magazine or in the event of the necessity of creating by the contest's sponsors a press release announcing the results of the judging.

Michael Martone was born in Fort Wayne, Indiana, where from an early age he entered contests and sweepstakes he found advertised on the side panels of cereal boxes or listed in his local newspaper. Often, he was required to collect and send box tops from specially marked packages or proof-of-purchase seals, along with filled-in application forms. He would fill out pads of entry forms by hand to comply with the instruction in the fine print against photocopying or employing any means of mechanical reproduction. He wrote his name, address, and phone number over and over so that any time he picked up a pen or pencil he automatically began to print (the instructions always asked that he print) his contact information. His mother tracked his winnings. She kept scrapbooks she labeled *My Achievements*, where she taped in copies of coupons and receipts sent to Martone to redeem the prizes and awards, the congratulatory letters, and the original game rules. After all those blank entry blanks, Martone gravitated to the contests asking for a bit of his creative effort, a drawing or a brief essay, as well as the completion of the requisite entry forms. The essays were his favorite since he couldn't draw to save his life. The rules always asked for the submission to be of a certain word length, 100 words or less, or 250 words or less. That formulation of words in the guidelines always disturbed Martone's mother, who was an English teacher. She corrected the instructions, in red pencil no less, inserting "fewer" above the crossed-out "less." Martone liked the puzzle of the number of words, liked using every word allowed, liked to imagine that someone somewhere actually read his little essays, counted the words as he or she did so, even though he suspected, quite early, that his efforts were simply more elaborate entry forms. The winners, runners-ups, and honorable mentions were all, no doubt, selected by the usual method of random drawing. Martone became adept at the form. His specialty was the use of words compounded by employing a hyphen such as "proof-of-purchase" or "runners-up." The grafting counted as one word instead of two or three. In high school he obsessively entered such essay contests sponsored by civic organizations and church groups, soliciting his thoughts on patriotic themes, good citizenship, personal health, and public sanitation. He often won contests and was invited to luncheon meetings of attentive Rotarians, Lions, Zontas, and Veterans who appreciated the brevity of the winning essays. Years later, Martone is still entering contests, writing tiny paragraphs of prose. Now, oddly, these contests require that he pay to enter, more like a state lottery but with better odds. Martone likes using long titles. He figures those words don't count. Today, he writes on his computer. It has a word count feature. He pushes one button, and he automatically knows where he stands. His mother no longer has to count the words by hand, looking up at him at the end and whispering, "Fewer." ◆

Kissing for Klutzes

JUDY MILLAR

*To kiss: the act of touching one's lips
to someone else's in a show of affection*

Kissing sounds simple, but as a teenage klutz, I knew it would not come easily to me.

Spatial awareness has always been a stretch. When I execute forward motion in proximity to other objects, bad things happen. Bad things happened to the trunk of a parked Buick when I was learning to ride a bike. Bad things happened to a pommel horse when I attempted a scissors dismount in Gymnastics class. So I knew bad things would happen if I ever bumped braces with anybody—and I didn't even wear braces.

I was terrified to try kissing anyway, thanks to Miss Struthers. She was the meanest gym teacher who ever bounced a basketball. When she wasn't carrying on about a damaged box horse, she was teaching her own merciless version of sex ed. Her mantra? *Kissing causes pregnancy.* Exactly how kissing did this she left deliberately vague. Fortunately, I had a good imagination. Although I couldn't make out much of the illustration on the screen at the front of the room, I surmised that the tube going up from the man's testicle must somehow patch into his saliva ducts. *Yuck.* I scratched kissing off my "to do" list.

Fortunately, Rosie Disano set me straight. Rosie was our neighborhood "sexpert." Not because she'd actually had any sex, but because she was Italian. Everybody knew Italians were hot-blooded. Rosie swore that Miss Struthers was just trying to scare us. According to her, you could not get pregnant from kissing; you could only get pregnant if the man drilled a hole into your leg.

Rosie's grasp of the mechanics of it all seemed a little vague—she may have been only half Italian. In any case, leg drilling didn't seem like the sort of thing that could happen by accident, so I decided to experiment with kissing, being careful to avoid anyone carrying a power tool.

My first experiment's name was Jimmy Hochstead. He was short. *Very* short. I couldn't picture anyone that short even lifting a power tool. I never knew what Jimmy saw in me, although his straight-on view of my chest may have played a part. But I knew what I saw in him. He had a car. Well, not much of a car, but it had four wheels. And two doors. And a booster seat on the driver's side. So Jimmy didn't look all that short behind the steering wheel—which is why I insisted we see *Bonnie and Clyde* at the drive-in. There was less chance of anyone I knew spotting us and deciding Judy and Jimmy were a duo. Plus, a car afforded privacy for possible kissing.

Nothing much happened, on screen or off, until Bonnie and Clyde graduated from small-time heists to full-fledged bank robberies. Things were just heating up when I realized I needed to visit the washroom. On my way back, I stumbled on the uneven ground and collapsed onto the dirt path in a moaning heap, clutching my sprained ankle. A Good Samaritan rushed over to help me and began to shout: "Does anyone know this girl?" His girlfriend must have notified the concession booth staff. To my horror, management responded by turning on full field floodlights just as Jimmy came forward to claim me. I limped back to his car with more eyes on me than on the bank manager Clyde had just shot in the face.

That spoiled the moment for me. Not for Jimmy. Being my knight in shining armor had inflamed him. I barely had my throbbing ankle propped up on the dashboard when he moved in for a kiss. What he lacked in stature he channeled into propulsion. Plus, he had lips like concrete curbs.

Worse yet, he was a presser. He pressed so hard his incisors made indents in my upper lip. Somehow I managed to back out of the lip-lock. Rosie Disano had never warned me about any of this so I had no countermoves planned. When Jimmy honed back in, I did the only thing I could think of. I bit down hard on his lower lip.

"What the hell did you do that for?" he hollered. I said the only thing I could think of: "I'm a klutz. My teeth slipped."

I've since decided kissing is an art form. Art requires practice. Over the years I've put in my share. These days, hardly anyone gets hurt. ◆

Gained in Translation:
A Real-Life Play in One Act

MARK BUDMAN

Set in the Interpreter's home office in present-day America. The Interpreter just hung up the phone, and his hands are shaking.

Ring-Ring

The Interpreter (in English): This is Michael, the Russian Interpreter. Ready to take the call.

The Agency's Operator (in English): US military.

The Interpreter (in English): Roger that.

The Agency's Operator (in English): You are connected.

The Interpreter (in English): I'm Michael, your Russian Interpreter. May I help you?

The Female Officer (in English): I'm Lieutenant Bridgett Smith. We will be talking to Ukraine about a lost vehicle.

The Interpreter (in English): Ma'am, the Interpreter is a *Russian* one. The Interpreter doesn't speak Ukrainian.

FO (in English): I called them a few minutes ago. They said *nyet*. That's Russian for "no," right?

The Interpreter (in English): Some basic words sound the same in Russian and Ukrainian, ma'am, but the Interpreter won't be able to sustain an intelligent conversation using only basic words.

FO (in English): What do you suggest?

The Interpreter (in English): The Interpreter suggests to try them.

FO (in English): I will connect.

Ring-Ring

Female Voice (in Russian or Ukrainian): Hello.

The Interpreter (in broken Ukrainian): Do you speak Russian?

Female Voice (in Russian): Yes.

The Interpreter (in Russian): This is US military calling. I am Michael, your English interpreter. Lieutenant Bridgett Smith is looking for a lost vehicle.

Female Voice (in Russian): Huh? This a private apartment. Did you just call me before? I already said "no."

The Interpreter (in English): Huh? This a private apartment. Did you just call me before? I already said "no."

FO (in English): Huh? I was given this number.

The Interpreter (in Russian): Huh? I was given this number.

FO (in English): We are sorry to bother you.

The Interpreter (in Russian): We are sorry to bother you.

Female Voice (in Russian): We love America.

The Interpreter (in English): We love America.

FO (in English): Thank you.

The Interpreter (in Russian): Thank you.

Disconnect

FO (in English): Maybe I misdialed. Maybe I'll dial again.

The Interpreter (in English): It's your call, ma'am.

Ring-Ring

Female Voice (in Russian): Hello.

The Interpreter (in Russian): This is US military. I am Michael, your English interpreter. We are looking for a lost vehicle.

Female Voice (in Russian): Huh? This a private apartment. Did you just call, twice? What the fuck?

The Interpreter (in English): Huh? This a private apartment. Did you just call, twice? What the fuck?

Disconnect

FO (in English): She didn't say that she loves America this time?

The Interpreter (in English): No, ma'am, she did not. Is there anything else the Interpreter can help you with?

FO (in English): No, thanks. You were very good.

The Interpreter (in English): Thank you for using our interpreting agency.

Disconnect

The Interpreter gets up from his chair and heads for the bathroom, unzipping.

Ring-Ring

The Interpreter runs back, half-zipped.

The Interpreter (in English): This is Michael, the Russian Interpreter. Ready to take the call.

The Agency's Operator (in English): Mental Health Center of Denver. Grievance resolution center. Warning: The client is pissed mightily.

The Interpreter (in English): Acknowledged.

The Agency's Operator (in English): You are connected.

Female Voice (in Russian): Aaaaaaaaaaaaaaaaaaaaaaah.

The Interpreter (in English): Aaaaaaaaaaaaaaaaaaaaaaah. ◆

And a Free Box of Forty

SUZANNE STREMPEK SHEA

I left home for college with the normal amount of angst about meeting new people. But I quickly found out I had an easy icebreaker.

"You're from where?" the strangers would ask.

"Palmer, Mass."

They would nod blankly, as you do when you meet someone from a place you've never heard of but want to appear as if you have. Then they would stop: "Wait—why do I know that name?"

I learned to stand there and let them figure it out, which they usually did— that they knew of my tiny western Massachusetts town because since earliest memory they'd seen its name printed on the side of baby-blue cartons stashed beneath the bathroom sink. My hometown, and its most famous product, had sneaked into their psyches.

Tampax. Palmer, Mass.

Actually, the line should have read "Three Rivers, Mass.," the village in Palmer where the plant towered on a ledge above the Chicopee River, eleven houses down from the one in which I grew up.

I passed the place nearly every day of my young life. I cannot pinpoint when I realized the unusual and highly personal nature of the things made within those brick walls, but I have always felt a kinship with kids who grew up in the shadows of offbeat manufacturers.

I once met a guy whose town thrived because of a condom business, and a woman whose high school class partied next to the local brassiere factory. As embarrassed teens, they, too, had lied when out-of-town dates asked what was made in that building over there, always giving an answer like "shovels." Brothers and sisters they were to me.

Tampax was just another part of Main Street, part of the scenery, this huge structure with its odd series of angled roofs. For fifty-five years it turned out feminine hygiene products, and took in several generations of employees who'd otherwise have been commuting far for work in our largely rural area. Their cars and trucks jammed the parking lot. They busied Main Street, walking at lunch for a bite at Dominick's, or to do errands at the drugstore and bank.

Get a job at Tampax and you were set for life—after all, you were making something that was never going out of style.

Everybody I knew worked there, had once worked there, or knew it was possible to work there.

And for three months, I, too, worked there, spending my first summer back from college hunched from 7 a.m. to 3 p.m. at a noisy and lightning-fast packing machine, feeding into its ever-hungry maw the fashionably shaded purse containers that came free in every box and that offered a discreet way for customers to carry along a pair of products. When my machine froze, a stern Portuguese woman materialized with the right combination of impressive whacks and shoves to get those Super Pluses rolling freely past once again.

On the way to lunch on the common across the street, my line-neighbor Elmo and I would stop to admire the glass case displaying Tampax around the world, boxes labeled in the languages of exotic places where the tampons had traveled and we could only dream of visiting. Once a month, need 'em or not, female or not, we were handed our employee bonus: a free box of forty.

The job also gave me a decent salary, a great reverence for those who do line work, and the determination to avoid it. I also received an eye-opening regarding my father, who for thirty-seven years, beginning in his teens, had toiled in the filth of the Uniroyal tire factory on another rocky ledge eighteen miles downriver. How could he do the same exact boring thing every single day, I found myself wondering for the first time.

"Everybody has to do something for work," is how I remember him putting it. "I'm lucky to have a job."

Thanks to my dad's employment, my sister and I annually were shod in discounted pairs of rubber-soled Keds. And, whenever Lincoln's head could be seen on a penny inserted into worn treads, our Plymouth Fury III likewise was fitted with new footwear from the company store.

Though necessary in modern life, shoes and tires pale next to tampons as conversation starters. But my factory time was a summer's laugh, while my father's was so many daylight hours grayed by lampblack. Which probably is why he never really wanted to start a conversation about it anyhow. ◆

You and That Mad Cow

LEAH WILLIAMS

You're at the blood drive, avoiding the nurses' calls of "Next?" as you wait for your spouse, who has been ushered into a cardboard cell. The nurses don't believe you lived in England during a mad cow scare in the mid-'90s and are forbidden to donate. They think you're a coward. Which you are. But not because you won't give blood. You're terrified that the Red Cross still thinks some dread disease is eating holes in your brain bit by bit, like some demonic caterpillar.

You noted the symptoms on WebMD the night before: impaired vision, loss of coordination, dementia.

"You have all of those," said your spouse.

There are no tests you can take. But there is some comfort: If you die after a suspicious spiral into lunacy, doctors can study your brain to determine whether you were (a) old, (b) infected, or (c) an Alzheimer's victim. It seems the medical establishment can confidently affirm two things about what they call variant Creutzfeldt-Jakob disease: 1. It's fatal. 2. They know jack shit about it.

You wish you could reassure yourself that you'd chosen the period of your exposure, your junior year in England, to become a vegetarian. Instead, you know you were at the cafeteria's burger bar daily. Usually, you weren't this big of a carnivore. But this is a country where they fry toast. Where they add corn to pizza. Where everything tastes boiled. No wonder you imbibed a lifetime of cows in one year.

And you weren't exactly dining in a premier establishment. You think those dreaded words to yourself, "college cafeteria," and know you were consuming a level of beef that doesn't earn a letter grade. You picture a farmer squinting at bleary-eyed, mange-covered, stumbling cows. "Simon," he says to his partner, swatting flies. "Send those ones over to the school. They'll take 'em."

Once you actually read a newspaper, you determined that current events were, in fact, relevant to your life. You avoided the burger bar, raided the vending machines. You were proud of this fortitude, which you managed to sustain until the night of the university's ball, which students had been raving about for months. "They always get some great band," those in the know had told you.

When you heard the choice, Right Said Fred of "I'm Too Sexy" fame, you were shocked, but far too amused not to go. Which is why you saw that grill with burgers at the event, and smelled the tempting, forbidden scent, and remembered the weeks of deprivation and mushy food, and started salivating, and thought, "Just this once." And you know that's the one, that's the burger that will kill you.

But not yet. Tonight you get to hear your husband praised by nurses when he nearly faints—the wimp. You feel your stomach gurgling. You dimly recall headlines about recent beef scares: millions of pounds recalled, healthy heads on sick cows.

Urban legends for sure.

"Honey," you say. "Let's go get some burgers." ◆

Pillars of the Community

JOSH COUVARES

Some people write vows like they're talking to their dog. You're so sweet; you're always happy to see me; you wait for me at the door after a long day of work; you're such a good boy, you know that, Max? Who's the good boy? You're the good boy.

These probably aren't the thoughts a person should be thinking while sitting with family listening to the priest tell us why we're gathered here today, but I am.

"Marriage," the priest says. "It is the promise of hope between a man and a woman."

Hope? I didn't think there was any left by the time you get married.

"You all here are making a vow as well," the priest says. "A vow to be there for this beautiful couple."

But I can't even tell you their names. Some guy and my cousin, Lydia or Lindsey—not sure which. People should be banned from writing their own vows. It should be a felony offense. Stick to the script or risk serving twenty years in maximum security. Because imagine this: What if all you've got to say is, "You're the nicest person I've ever met"? What do you do then? Call up the divorce lawyer the next day and take the wedding debt as a wash?

"When they need someone to celebrate with them, to guide them."

I notice this white spot while the priest's talking. More of a smudge, really. I stick my thumb in my mouth and try to wet it out of my pants' leg.

An old girlfriend, she showed me how to get out stains like this. I'd kiss her when she was putting on her makeup and it'd end up on the collar of my shirt. She'd lick a piece of the fabric and rub it against the makeup stain. Worked best on suit jackets.

"To console them, to help them—all of you are a part of their journey."

I'm working on my stain, and I shouldn't say old girlfriend. For one, she's younger than I am. Another, she's my *current* girlfriend.

"Now," says the priest. "We'd like to have Anne come up to say a few words."

But it's not my aunt Anne because she's still in the row in front of me. Must be the groom's family. This is what happens when two Irish families marry. You got an Aunt Anne? Now you've got two. Two Uncle Bills? Now you've got four. Ten aunts and uncles? Now you've got twenty-seven.

Whichever Anne this is, she's not mic'ed so I can't hear. People near me turn toward the voice, but I know none of them can see her because there's this pillar in the way. I keep working on my stain. This Anne's probably quoting from the Bible, "Love is patient and kind"—that kind of thing. Nothing interesting.

All I can see are the bridesmaids, which isn't half bad. Anne's talking about love and I'm imagining how the girl on the end would look naked—Father, you, in the front by the groom, forgive me.

Why bother with the fuss of weddings? If I have to tie the knot I'm going to city hall—which I imagine would be a lot like the DMV: long lines, too much paperwork, and you leave feeling worse than when you came in.

"By the power invested in me by the state of Massachusetts, I now pronounce you man and wife. You may now kiss the bride."

Everyone waits for the kiss. It's like the millisecond between turning a tuning knob on a guitar and the string snapping. I can't see anything because there's this mountain of a pillar blocking my view, but my mom, she's next to me, and she cranes her neck to get a better view. I can feel the smile that's growing across her face. I try to imagine why: Is it because my cousin and her finally-husband are embracing for the first time? To get married and have a big wedding—there's a kind of defiance. All the generations of bad marriages, the unknowable of the future, but despite that they're promising, "Hey, I'm not leaving until I'm six feet under."

A promise can be broken but it's still a promise—it's hope that something can last even when nothing seems to. And for the rest of us, we get to witness it.

My mom's smiling so much I think there's a tear in her eye. ◆

What You Need to Feed Your Baby

SUSAN LERNER

✓ **An ability to idealize.** Imagine your not-yet-conceived infant blissfully suck-ling. Fantasize that your nursing infant will complete you in the way of lovers.

✓ **A vow to be the perfect mother**—nothing like your distant mother who tried to breastfeed once and gave up.

✓ **A move to a new city** just after your husband knocks you up, one where you know no one.

✓ **Books.** Buy every book written by about breastfeeding. Note the only sug-gestion common to every text: Never wash your nipples with soap.

✓ **A goal.** The American Academy of Pediatrics pushes for breastfeeding a full year. Recoil at glossy ads for "Enfamil." Promise yourself you will feed your growing fetus nothing but your own perfect milk until he or she packs for college.

✓ **Obsession.** Examine your knockers whenever you change clothes. Admire the heft, curves, and the way you fill out a sweater.

✓ **Rage.** After delivery, eye-dagger the too-cheerful nurse who exclaims to baby, "Time for lunch!" Feel pain knuckle up your throat as your daughter screams and turns away. Stare in horror as the nurse flicks baby's cheek. Resist impulse to hit nurse as she pinches your nipple.

✓ **A tendency toward depression.** Cry during baby's screaming jags. Leave PJs on for days. Call nurse, who insists everything will be fine and reminds you not to use soap on your nipples. Call La Leche woman, who reminds you not to use soap on your nipples. Hurl phone across the room.

✓ **An ability to go numb** when strangers handle your hooters. Discover that a nationally known lactation consultant lives only two hours away. Allow hope to bloom as your husband chauffeurs. Feel optimism ebb as she leads you with Birkenstocked feet into an office with walls covered in handmade decorations. Take off your shirt. Zone out as she pokes and pinches. Leave with instructions. Purchase from her capsules of fenugreek, an oregano-like herb. Line your bra with cabbage leaves.

✓ **Days without sleep.** Your udders are your identity. The capsules have given you pizza-breath; your boobs belong in a garden.

✓ **A desire to get sexy with plastic.** Purchase a Supplemental Nursing System that hangs from your neck and drains through slender plastic tubes you tape to your nipples.

✓ **A perfect combination** of laughing and crying that you dub a craugh. Smile through tears when your husband says you look like a porno circus performer. Roll your eyes at his request for a naked dance. Tear up when baby screams at tape and plastic in her mouth. Rip tape from nipples in one punishing motion. Rent electric breast pump. Position its plastic cones on your jugs. Do not laugh when your husband extolls your Wonder Woman boobs. Widen your eyes as machine stretches your nipples like rubber bands. Descend into despair at their tiny offering of milk. Sob.

✓ **Timing.** Know when to cry uncle! Hiccup through tears and send hubby for Enfamil.

✓ **Wild shame that will fuck you hard.** Join a New Mothers group. Watch other women hike up their shirts to feed their placid babies. Try to quiet your daughter's screams. Grow hot in the face as you pull a bottle from your diaper bag.

✓ **A good pediatrician.** Call baby's doctor to report her shrieking. Tell about baby's vomiting. Say that your floors are carpeted in heaps of puke-soaked clothes. Disbelieve "colic." Listen as she says, "Call back when the spit-up is strong enough to hit the wall." Do your own hitting of the wall. Wail.

✓ **Cases of Tide.**

✓ **Savings.** Toss out Enfamil. Buy different formulas. Toss out barely used cans. Make appointment with specialist. Let relief wash over you when the doctor diagnoses Milk-Soy Protein Intolerance. Take fleeting pleasure that he's confirmed you're not crazy. Shell out one hundred dollars for imported prescription formula. Beat yourself up because—breastfeeding. Steep in guilt.

✓ **Timing:** Know when to leave the party. Return to New Mothers group. Notice other mothers' brushed hair and lipstick. Ponder contents of your diaper bag: bottles. Ponder contents of their diaper bags: diapers. Go home. Weep.

✓ **Perseverance.** Watch your daughter grow despite everything.

✓ **A small amount of mathematics.** Allow tragedy + time to = comedy. Chuckle as you tell friends how your toddler once left half a Cheerio. Pretend to be your girl when she was a toddler and joke: *I'm so full, I couldn't possibly finish.*

✓ **Perspective.** Reflect on the kaleidoscope of your successes and failures. Forgive your mammaries. Forgive yourself. Forgive your mother. Your grown daughter, strong and whip-smart, still needs you. Be with her. It's not too late. ◆

An Angry Letter to Starbucks

KATHRYN FITZPATRICK

Dear Howard Schultz,

Sometimes when I'm feeling classy, I'll go to Starbucks instead of Dunkin' for my medium vanilla iced coffee. Starbucks is the bourgeois answer to the chain-breakfast establishment, and sometimes it feels nice to interact with the upper crust. Starbucks is for people who drive shiny cars and have retirement plans, while Dunkin' is the standby favorite of blue-collar folks who flip their underwear inside out instead of doing laundry. At any of the 12,000 Starbucks establishments nationwide, you can expect the same thing: a modern greige color pallet, an innocuous adult contemporary soundtrack, Hillary Clinton wannabes who keep their children on leashes, baristas who look like they #StoodWithStandingRock. There is one feature in this progressive young American's haven, however, that does not belong.

Mr. Schultz, the food at Starbucks is shit. Nothing in the dumpy display case ever looks appetizing, and I'm sure it's inedible, too. The sandwiches always look flat, like they've been crushed by the weight of the national debt; the pastries look glazed over and depressed. And those little round, shriveled things that you're advertising all of a sudden? I have no clue what they are, but they look like undescended testicles and someone needs to call the censorship bureau on you because they freak me out.

Mr. Schultz, why do you insist on cutting corners in the culinary department? I know you have plenty of funding kicking around, because every Christmas you roll out a new line of mildly festive, nondenominational cups to celebrate a slew of winter holidays. Let me tell you something, Mr. Schultz: These intricately-designed, 100-percent recycled red paper cups will probably just end up in the blowhole of a whale, so really, you're wasting your time. And according to capitalist doctrine, time is money. And I want to spend my money on a bacon, egg, and cheese that doesn't look like it's going to be recalled by the USDA for listeria contamination.

Give me a Starbucks that focuses its efforts on locally sourced, regional favorites. A Starbucks that supports local shops and farms while simultaneously monopolizing the market, putting every family-owned coffeehouse in a ten-mile radius out of business. When I'm at Starbucks in New York, I want the best goddamn bagel I've ever had. When I'm at Starbucks in California, I want some disgusting vegan options. In Minnesota, give me some artery-clogging casserole covered in tater tots, or whatever they eat up there in the land God forgot about. When I'm in your founding state of Washington, Mr. Shultz, give me a Danish so orgasmic it will cure my seasonal depression.

I'll admit, I'm no economist. I don't handle large sums of money or study the patterns of people who walk through your contemporary Plexiglas doors. I am nothing but a lowly bank teller and college student. But I implore you to change your company, Mr. Schultz. The ball is in your court. And according to Title IX, we can both play the game.

Sincerely,
One Hangry Customer

◆

Don't Bed Down with a Canine

JIM SHEA

"If you lie down with dogs, you get up with fleas."

You would think for this reason alone, the vast majority of dog owners would be reluctant to allow Fido to zonk out in their bed.

Guess again.

According to the American Kennel Club, between 42 and 45 percent of dog owners share a bed with their dog, or dogs.

I have no idea if these folks get up with fleas or not. Maybe they dab on a little Top Spot before bedtime, or don a collar, or take special baths.

Seems like a lot of trouble.

In our house, we do not bed down with the hound. He is not only canine non grata in the bed, but upstairs as well. Once the lights go out, his job description is lower level security.

There is sound reasoning behind this approach. You let a dog in your bed and the next thing you know he's sleeping on the furniture. And then one day you walk into the family room and there he is, parked in the recliner watching *Dog Whisperer* reruns on the flat screen.

There are, of course, a whole host of other potential problems, such as how it is decided which side of the bed the dog gets.

My assumption had been that a dog always occupied the foot of the bed. Apparently, this is not the case. Apparently, many people let a sleeping dog lie anywhere it wants. Does anyone else see the problems here?

I mean, it's sobering enough to encounter human morning breath. One can only imagine the shock of being greeted by the funky blowback of a bed partner that rarely, if ever, brushes, flosses, or gargles. And let's not even go into licking.

Or consider the other alternative. You roll over, open your eyes, and find yourself facing a dog's business end. Is this really the way you want to start your day?

And what if it goes off? Dogs possess the internal combustion to turn a filched scrap of forbidden table food into a major air quality situation. These emissions are not only capable of causing temporary blindness, palpitations, and shortness of breath, but can also require the frequent repainting of bedroom walls.

Finally, there is the matter of dreaming: Dogs dream all the time. You can tell when they are dreaming because they whimper and whine and move their legs to suggest they are running. Sometimes they are dreaming of chasing rabbits or cats. Sometimes they are dreaming of the cute little poodle down the street.

If you are unfortunate, your dreaming dog will catch up with the cute little poodle down the street. And you thought the business end was a bad way to greet the new day. ◆

Cocktail Time

KIM ADDONIZIO

Everyone thinks that being a writer disposes one toward heavy drinking. Like all ideas about writers, this statement contains some truth, adulterated with gossip and the romantic fantasies of young aspiring writers. The truth is that we spend an inordinate amount of time at our work, which means we spend our time alone, in a room of our own if we're lucky, and in the worlds in our heads. Depending on your feelings about solitude, and your own inner life, you may understand why some of us enjoy the company of spirits.

If you think it's amazing that humans have up to thirty feet of intestines coiled in our bodies, think about the galaxies and planets, the supernovas and nebulae and wormholes that exist in writers' heads. If we want an occasional cocktail to help us cope with the vast- ness of space, don't give us a hard time. Go get a wheatgrass enema and drink your herbal tea. Be healthy and happy, and do not dwell on the past, the future, imag- inary people in parallel universes, or what might have been. See how much work you get done.

My friend Elizabeth invented a drink she called the E-tini. Once, when I was asked to contribute a rec- ipe to a food and drink anthology, I included her drink and invented my own, the K-tini. Here they both are:

Two Quick & Dirty Drink Recipes to Get You Quickly Dirty

The E-tini

Into a glass, flask, juice jar, paper cup, hollowed coconut shell, or other suitable container such as cupped hands (having a partner for this last will prove to be useful), pour:

⅓ Absolut Vanilla vodka, fresh from the freezer
⅓ cold orange juice
⅓ cold pineapple juice

Top with a floater of the Absolut. Do not stir. Drink immediately.

The E-tini tastes like a Dreamsicle. It's simple, refreshing, and full of sugar, but you can feel good that you are drinking two kinds of juice. If you wish to bypass feeling good and go straight to feeling fucked up, try the K-tini.

The K-tini

1. Open freezer and remove any hard, alcoholic beverage.
2. Unscrew cap.
3. Open mouth and apply to bottle.
4. Swallow as many times as possible on a single inhale.

Wine from the refrigerator or cupboard may be substituted for 1); in that case, however, the characteristic and oft-mentioned "kick" of the K-tini can't be experienced. Wine is for wannabes. The K-tini is the drink for those in the know, those who are sick with thirst, whose demons are swarming. Your demons snicker at wine, at lite beer, at bitters and soda. Give them what they clamor for: Give them K-tinis. Feel so fucked up you fall to the floor, hitting your head on your marble counter. When you wake up, put on your sexiest online Victoria's Secret purchase and dance wildly before your full-length mirror, then collapse sobbing into a pile of soiled underwear, weeping because there is no one to see how hot you look. Decide to go to the bar; have another K-tini before you leave, then get behind the wheel. Don't stop for the car you sideswipe or the kitten you mow down. Drive! Drive! Your true love is waiting for you. You'll be together forever, as soon as you hit that tree. ◆

The Bad Passenger

SARAH WESLEY LEMIRE

As a sea of red brake lights glows in front of me, I slam down on my own brakes in anticipation of a quick stop. From behind the steering wheel my husband shoots me a tired look and asks, "How's that invisible passenger brake working out for you over there?"

"Not very well," I reply. "Maybe we should get it looked at."

I'm aware that in terms of riding shotgun, I'm about as fun as sharing toenail clippers at a fungus convention. But it's not my fault. I suffer from Episodic Automobile Freak-Out Disorder, or EAFOD [pronounced eee-*faw*-d], as it's more commonly known.

Though largely ignored by the medical community, EAFOD is a rare but serious condition where afflicted persons frequently suffer from wide-eyed facial flinching, profuse sweating, uncontrollable spasms of the arms and legs, involuntary verbal outbursts like "*WatchoutWatchoutWatchout*," along with the indiscriminate use of four-letter words and compulsive side mirror checking, all which occur while traveling as a passenger in a car.

It's incurable.

Initial onset occurred in my early adulthood, after spending a significant amount of time in the car with my brother, David.

No ride with Dave was ever complete without at least one near-death experience. An honors graduate from the Lindsay Lohan School of Driving, he had the uncanny ability to sift through his entire CD collection while changing lanes at eighty miles an hour.

Also, an attentive conversationalist, he liked to make prolonged, steady eye contact with me as I sat, rigid with apprehension, in the passenger seat. I rarely returned the favor as I was too preoccupied with looking forward and pointing out roadside attractions like stoplights and pedestrians.

When riding together I habitually found myself saying his name in some combination of inquiry and terror. "Dave? Dave? Dave? Dave! *Dave! Dave!*

DAVE!" Then after a swerve and catastrophic near-miss, he'd calmly look over at me and say, "What?"

Now, years later, my brother still becomes irritated if I mention his driving and the words "primal fear" in the same sentence, and then pointedly reminds me of the time that, itching to use my newly minted driver's license, I insisted on driving him to the mall.

At cruising speed, I hit a large pool of standing water in the middle of the road and lost control of the car. Like a scene from *The Matrix*, we stared at one another in slow motion as the car did a series of whooshing, 360-degree spins before eventually coming to a stop beneath a billboard that read, "Jesus Loves You."

It would be years before Dave agreed to ride with me again.

In addition to my passenger disability, I also suffer from EAFOD's sister affliction, Episodic *Airplane* Freak-Out Disorder. It's a relatively mild case considering there are only a few things that really bother me about flying, including check-in, boarding, ascending, descending, and every moment in between.

The good news is that I've found a treatment that helps manage my symptoms.

It's a remedy that I like to call "Xan Grigio," which consists of a single Xanax washed down with a liberal amount of white wine. My prescription bottle specifically warns against this because it can apparently cause drowsiness, difficulty concentrating, and impaired thinking.

Well, *helloooo*?

If I actually wanted to think about flying 32,000 feet above the earth in a soup can, I wouldn't need Xan Grigio in the first place. Impairment is not a side effect, it's the objective. Without it, the flight attendants would have to pry me off the exit door, where I'd be clinging like one of those suction-cup Garfield dolls you see in the back windows of cars.

Of course, you should never try this at home, and certainly don't cite me if you do. Equally, if my doctor is reading this, I just made up all that stuff about Xanax and wine. Wait, what?

As for my brother, he lives abroad and will probably never read this. If he does, however, I want to state for the record that he is the best, safest driver on the road, no matter what country he's in, just as long as it's not this one. ◆

An Objective Look at My Seven Graduate School Rejections

CHELSEA BIONDOLILLO

1. **University of Iowa versus my rejection for entry into the Jean Jacket Club in the third grade**

   The jean jacket thing was worse. Sure, I would have loved to have attended U of I; are you kidding? But their rejection rate for MFA applicants is traditionally around 98 percent, while the two most popular girls in grade school let all of the girls with jean jackets into the club except me.

2. **University of New Mexico versus William Golding's twenty rejections by publishers for Lord of the Flies**

   This one is going to have to go to UNM. The university wasn't even ranked when I applied, so when it said no, it hurt in a more visceral way. Maybe if my writing sample hadn't included so many occurrences of the word "visceral"? Too late now. In contrast, Golding had already published a book of poems by the time everyone was turning down his novel. And it's true, UNM has suddenly jumped to a top-ten ranked MFA program this year, which eases the pain a bit, but Golding went on to win a Nobel for Lord of the Flies—giving him the right to be smug and self-satisfied, if he so chose.

3. **University of Alabama versus Jesus's rejection by the Jews**

   Jesus totally gets this one. UA was originally one of my top choices, but getting this letter wasn't even close to being rejected by an entire people.

4. **University of Arizona versus the guy in front of me at the grocery store last week whose credit card was rejected**

   Man, he was really bummed. You know, you spend all this time shopping for things you really need, only to be told "sorry" at the end by some overworked, underpaid cashier who is wearing way too much eyeliner? You feel helpless: There's nothing you can do, unless you want to hold the line up while you try two more cards, or even worse, start subtracting things until you get down to however much cash you have on hand. But sorry, guy-at-the-store, losing a chance to study at my number-one choice was worse.

5. **Penn State versus George W. Bush's rejection to the University of Texas Law School in 1973**

Tie. To be fair, I don't think either of us cared at the time as much as we both should have.

6. **Notre Dame versus expulsion from the United Nations of the governing body known as the "Republic of China" in 1971**

Another tie. In this case, we both knew it was coming: I'm not Catholic and the UN wasn't communist. I know that's a huge oversimplification of very complex machinations, since the University of Notre Dame says Catholicism is not a criterion for attendance, but I have no doubt it contributed to my missing the short list of lucky admits. At least the ROC was told, personally, again and again—probably on masthead. All I got was an e-mail to check my status.

7. **Portland State University versus the International Astronomical Union's rejection of Pluto as a planet**

I know Pluto fans will disagree, but I am going to have to give this one to PSU, because Pluto itself could care less about being eighty-sixed from the oh-so-exclusive club of planets. Trust me, all you Pluto nuts, getting turned down by my hometown school, my safety school, and my last school —all in one letter —was worse. That letter meant another year of working retail, another year of trying to get some writing done on my thirty-minute lunch breaks, and another year of busting my ass for unpaid bylines. What does Pluto suffer? It's not like they're going to rename plutonium or that dumb dog. ◆

Nothing Happened

PAUL BECKMAN

"That's the reason you're not speaking anymore?"

"I'm talking to her. She's not speaking to me. That's the story. She'll have to speak first—then I'll speak to her."

"Tell me what happened."

"I told you. She did the same thing again."

"Humor me. Tell me."

"Well, I was in Stop and Shop because I had coupons. Usually I shop Big Y. I picked up a loaf of rye bread when that woman comes up to me and . . ."

"Your sister. That woman is your sister."

". . . That woman comes up to me and says, '*Seedless. How can you buy seedless?*' The first time that woman has spoke to me in five years she tells me I'm buying the wrong rye bread."

"Then what happened?"

"I says, 'Oy! Without my glasses they both look alike.' I put on my glasses and switched."

"But you don't like seeds in your rye bread. You say they get under your plate."

"I know, but I couldn't let *her* know that."

"Then?"

"She says, 'I thought you shopped that other place. Why are you slumming?' The mouth on her. I tell you. If I wasn't a lady. . . So I says 'Coupons.'"

"That's *all* you said?"

"That's all I had to say."

"Then what happened?"

"Nothing happened then."

"How can nothing happen? You're not talking again."

"Then nothing happened. I shopped and that woman went on her way."

"Your sister. Well. . .?"

"Look. I'm not saying anything bad. She bumped me in mustard."

"So?"

"I was looking at a jar of Gulden's when a cart bumps my cart and it's *her*."

"Anything break? Anyone hurt?"

"No."

"So what's the problem?"

"What's the problem, Mister?"

"I'm not Mister. I'm your nephew. What's the problem?"

"She says to me, 'For a few cents more you can get spicy.' So I get out my glasses and I switch for spicy."

"Spicy upsets your stomach."

"You think I'd let *her* know that?"

"So, 'cause she bumped you in mustard you're not talking."

"No. We're not talking 'cause she bumped me in mustard."

"Tell me."

"She says, 'So long as you're here you might as well come for coffee.' 'Another time maybe,' I says. 'It's time for me to go home for lunch.' And she says, 'So come for coffee and lunch. I'll get a can tuna,' she says. So I says, 'Don't get bread. Bread I have right here—a nice rye.' So she says, 'I can't eat that, the seeds get under my plate.' So can you believe that?"

"So that's why you're not talking again?"

"Of course not. So I come up to her house for coffee and maybe a bite and right off she apologizes for the mess and the house is so clean you could eat off the floor."

"So what happened? After five years you're at least talking. What possibly could have happened?"

"So I come into the kitchen while she starts the tuna and she says to me, 'Coffee?' 'Sure,' I says. Well, the water boils and she puts the instant in the cup and pours the water about two-thirds full. Listen, I make instant for myself, don't get me wrong. But for company I perc. I know. This is for a sister. Good enough."

"So?"

"So she gives me the cup of instant and goes back to mixing the tuna and I says, 'I'd like a full cup of coffee—not a half cup,' and she says, 'It's not a half cup—I left room for cream.' I tell her I take mine black so I'd like a full cup, please. So she says, 'So you'll have another.' I tell her it's not the same."

"Well, what happened then?"

"Nothing happened then."

"Then why aren't you talking again?"

" 'Cause nothing happened."

"If nothing happened why aren't you talking? What happened next?"

"Nothing happened. She mixed the tuna and I waited for her to fill my cup with more hot water."

"And . . .?"

"And nothing. She mixed. I waited. Then I got up and left."

"You just got up and left? After five years—why?"

"She says come up for coffee. She didn't say come up for a half cup. That I don't need her for. If she says come up for a cup of coffee she should at least give a cup of coffee if I come up."

"And that's why you're not talking?"

Listen, Mister, you know a better reason?" ◆

Barking

V. HANSMANN

There has been a turd under my therapist's recliner for a month. Every time she leans back, there it is. This turd is a byproduct of her teacup Yorkie, Sueño. I cannot take my eyes off it. Of course I do, but it doesn't take much for my focus to drift away from her benign countenance and drop to the silhouetted deposit below. What the fuck? Should I confront this distraction? What does it mean? And how do I know it's a turd?

It is a turd because I stepped on one in my stocking feet not too long ago and have had a mystical bond with Sueño's knuckle-size offerings ever since. Dolores, my therapist, insists her clientele remove their shoes. This has been the ritual since I began seeing her. When my right foot bore down on the canine waste unit, it rebounded as if repelled magnetically. The advantage of shoeless-ness is heightened sensitivity. The downside is increased vulnerability to dog shit. I glanced down at the carpet. What I saw was unmistakably a turd, just lying there slightly smooshed, like an unwrapped caramel. A bum's rush of associations hurtled through my brain. I tied my sneakers and left, shaking my head, "Jesus Christ, Dolores. Jesus fucking Christ" all the way to the elevator.

We go way back, Dolores and me. 1987. This is the fifth, no, sixth, of her "offices" I have sat in. She works out of her apartment and they have all been filled with drama, but only this last one has had dogs. She derives pleasure and comfort from Sueño, as she did from his predecessor, Skipper. The attention Dolores lavishes upon this creature makes her happy, yet Sueño wants more. I believe the dog exploits flattery to ensure the reliability of his food source.

If I take issue with this rogue turd, I will be asked how it makes me feel. Piece of shit = feelings. Is there something about the therapist/puppy relationship that threatens me? Does the turd under her chair rip the scab off some childhood trauma?

What I have come to really appreciate about Dolores is that she lets her life intrude into her practice. Her refusal to maintain customary therapeutic boundaries often places me in a position where intimacy cannot be avoided. I can react in the moment to an uncomfortable situation, either challenging her directly or leapfrogging the confrontation and landing on shards of resentment. Or I can step back and hold my tongue. In any event, I react. The hour we share is always provocative and over the years I have untangled skeins and skeins of bullshit.

When Dolores's door is closed and we are in session, if Sueño is on the other side, he will splay himself against the door repeatedly. The door is frosted glass so, in addition to whimper-and-smash, there is a visual. She opens the door and the dog spins in tiny circles then flies onto her lap, which, because of the recliner's recumbency, consists of her entire body.

I pretend Dolores is fully absorbed by my presence. I could challenge her on this, claim it reminds of my upbringing, and riff wildly. That would be the thing to do. I might insist that the dog occupy itself elsewhere when I am there. But where would the little thing go? Exiled to the bathroom? Stuffed into a smallish crate? Hell, this is my hour, my forty-five-minute therapeutic hour. Mine. If I banish the dog, or merely state my case firmly, there are bound to be repercussions. I might feel silly. I might feel guilty. I can't let the little dog get under my skin.

But he taunts me.

I have contemplated confronting Dolores with the dog's incontinence. For a month, I calculated and worried. The turd under her chair is a housekeeping problem and I don't live here. But if she had spinach between her teeth or toilet paper on her shoe or the hem of her skirt tucked into her waistband, I would tell her. ◆

An Open Letter to Future Ex-Boyfriends About How to Apologize for Wrongdoings at the End of Our Relationship

DANI BURLISON

Dear Future Ex-Boyfriends,

1. I will leave a note for you taped to the packaging scale at the Central Santa Rosa Library on a Tuesday afternoon. You must only retrieve it between 5:45 and 6 p.m. that evening. The note will have directions to our meeting place, including what time to arrive and a list of belongings you must return to me during our meeting. Follow the instructions carefully. Failure to do so could cost you your measly, sad excuse for a life.

2. As instructed on the note, you are to arrive at what appears to be a condemned meth house on a forested hillside in Monte Rio, on the south side of the Russian River. There is no cell service, electricity, or running water at the house so bring a bottle of San Pellegrino and a six-pack of gluten-free beer (for me, not you). Park approximately thirty yards down the dark, winding dirt driveway and enter the house through the back door, which will be marked with the fresh warm blood of a mysterious wild animal.

3. You will notice a short white stool next to the inside of the door. It will be covered with vibrant, fall-colored poison oak leaves. This is where you will place all of your belongings, including your car keys, wallet, cell phone, Chapstick, and every article of clothing you are wearing, including your socks. Any body jewelry must also be placed on the stool.

4. As you reach to lock the door behind you, you'll notice a black cotton strap hanging from the doorknob. This is a blindfold. Tie it around your head, covering your eyes completely, and stand there naked, waiting for further instructions.

5. At 8:17 p.m., when the house is completely dark (you won't know because of the blindfold, obviously), and a cool rush of air enters through the west-facing window in the kitchen, you will hear music playing upstairs. If you listen closely, you'll recognize the tunes as Nick Cave's *Murder Ballads*. The album will be on shuffle, so as to not offer you any predictability or familiarity while you stand there naked and blindfolded. When the first song ends, you may make your next move.

6. To your right, there will be a staircase with an unstable, shaky, and splintery wooden banister heading to where I'll be waiting for you. You may walk, facing forward, up the stairs. Don't walk too slowly, or the rats that have infested the house may claw and chew at your bare feet and legs. Once you reach the second-floor hallway, stop again and wait for further instructions from my assistant.

7. Soon, you will hear the sound of knives being sharpened. The rhythmic swish and swash of metal against the butcher steel will be your next cue. Turn your back to the sounds of the blade and begin walking backward. When you feel the fluttering of bat wings across your shoulders and a swarm of biting flies buzzing in your ears, you'll know that you've entered the room where I'm waiting to hear your bullshit.

8. This, ex-boyfriend, is where you begin to crawl, still backward, toward my feet. Yes, I know the floor is covered with broken glass. Yes, I know it hurts. Yes, I know you may cut your hands and knees. That's the point. I'll turn Nick Cave down at this point, and I'll stop sharpening the knives so we can both listen carefully as the shards of our broken relationship crunch and crack under your weight.

9. Only once you have reached my feet without a single complaint, moan, or teardrop—and only after you've returned the books I've loaned you and any miscellaneous earrings or undergarments I may have misplaced in your apartment or car—may you begin speaking to me. You'll have seven minutes. If your testimony is worthy, my assistant will return your belongings and release you. If not, we'll fight; me with my freshly sharpened cutlery and you with your bare, bloody hands.

Best of luck to you,
Dani

◆

Nasty Habits

TOM HAZUKA

Three friends and I spent our junior year of college in Switzerland, living in a large, lovely building with thirty other students from around the world. The Villa des Fougères was run by two American nuns, and it soon became apparent that their ideas about getting the most out of life rarely coincided with ours. For example, Sister Betty complained about the noise when we ingested multiple beers, hammered on our guitars, and howled the Rolling Stones's "Sweet Virginia" at 2 a.m. directly beneath her bedroom. Come on, who doesn't want to be lulled to sleep by the dulcet strains of four drunks bellowing "Got to scrape the shit right off your shoes"?

On another occasion, Sister Betty entered the room of a trio of girls known to the cognoscenti as "The Three Graces," only to discover that The Graces had adorned their walls with a slew of full frontal *Playgirl* photographs. In a state of willful blindness worthy of Sergeant Schultz from *Hogan's Heroes* ("I see nothing!"), Sister Betty said what she'd come to say before retreating with a Nixonian quantity of sweat flooding her upper lip.

For reasons unknown to me, most Villa residents were female. Interesting at all times, especially to a schmo like me who grew up with no sisters, this situation came in particularly handy when the girls raided their wardrobes to dress us guys in drag for Halloween. We were their living, breathing Ken dolls, stuffed into Barbie's unforgiving outfits.

Some Americans from other programs got into the costume spirit, and stopped by the Villa to fetch us for celebratory revels downtown. Sister Betty seemed to enjoy the motley queens for a night, the most outlandish of which might have been burly, 6-foot 4-inch Buddy Albert.

Buddy, Sister Betty, and a few other dudes in drag stood near the open door of my room, where I sat on my bed while a French girl who lived in the Villa was telling me to hold still as she applied lipstick to my unconvinced mouth. I couldn't see anyone, but heard every word of the conversation. Corinne finished the labial paint job, which felt greasy and weird. I wondered what kissing Corinne with lipstick on would feel like, especially while wearing a dress and black panty hose, and I'd gladly have stayed to find out if she shared my curiosity, but after a smile and a peck on the cheek she was gone.

OK, time to paint the town *rouge*. I was almost to my door when I heard the cross-dressing Buddy ask, out of nowhere and as seriously as if lives depended on it, "Sister, I was wondering, can a man who has a sex change operation become a nun?"

Veering mid-step before I reached the hall, I lurched against the wall and jammed both fists over my mouth. Shaking helplessly, muscles like tapioca, I slid to the floor fighting to stay silent.

Presumably because Sister Betty was speechless, Buddy pressed on without receiving a response. "Do you think if a priest gets the operation he'd be a nun by default?"

I could taste the lipstick on my quivering knuckles.

Somehow Buddy's sincerity never wavered. He likely had a head full of hashish, and what began as a twitting of Sister Betty had transformed into a personal theological inquiry.

"Do you think a certain amount of time would have to pass to, you know, make sure the transformation to a woman was fixed in their ID? Psychologically speaking, I mean."

"Buddy," Sister Betty said with a twinkle in her voice, "maybe your best option is to write to the Vatican. I could give you the address."

I managed to rise from the floor. I wiped the smeared lipstick off my face and walked into the hall.

Sister Betty gave a whistle worthy of a construction worker. "Nice legs," she told me. "You should wear a dress more often."

"Thanks," I said with a lame simper. *Touché*, I thought with grudging respect for Sister Betty's refusal to fold under pressure.

Not that my admiration caused me to warn her a week later, when The Three Graces taped Saran Wrap under her toilet seat. ◆

My Dachshund Talk Italian One Day

RENÉE E. D'AOUST

After David Sedaris

As the woman approached the Agno train station, Tootsie started wagging. Tootsie is an ambassador doggy. Since adopting her in America and bringing her home to Switzerland three months ago, more people have talked to me than in the last three years.

"*Salve.*" The woman and I had passed each other many times, but we'd never said "hello." The woman bent down to speak to Tootsie. "*Che bello! O bella?*"

"*Bella. Grazie.*" In Italian, as an added bonus, you can distinguish gender while giving or receiving a compliment.

"*Che carina.*" Tootsie sat, plopping her butt down. Her back is long and the distance to the ground is short, so the action of sitting ends abruptly with a jerk. Tootsie is black with two tan eyebrow marks, a tan diamond framing her snout, and tan-colored paws. Any training she has comes from previous owners we never met. I swelled with pride at her display of doggy manners. The woman pet one of Tootsie's long, floppy ears. Tootsie twisted and licked the woman's fingers.

The orange-colored train of the Ferrovia Lugano–Ponte Tresa line tooted and chugged by, on its regular 13:04 departure. The FLP is the only train I've ever seen with a smiley face painted on the front. The smiley face has no nose, but these things can be forgiven.

"*È un cucciolo?*"

"No."

People assume Tootsie is a puppy, probably because, as my husband Daniele says, "She's a foot and a half long and half a foot tall."

The woman stood and her perfume, a sweet wild rose, surrounded us. I picked up Tootsie and held her forward, so the woman could keep petting her.

"*Quanti anni ha?*"

"Ha sei ani."

The woman took two steps back. She narrowed her focus into a Swiss frown. The frown is judgmental and corrective, meaning you've done or said something wrong, and you should know what it is. When I first moved to Switzerland, I made a game of counting Swiss frowns. One day, between claiming the wrong train seat, eating cold spaghetti from Tupperware on the bus, and walking on the wrong grass, I made it up to ten.

Maybe she hadn't heard me. I repeated myself loudly and with more confidence. *"Ha sei ani."* I patted Tootsie's rump.

The woman picked up her black leather bag and walked away. Tootsie tried to lick my face, but I didn't let her. I set her down, and we walked home. My Tube of Fur waddles when she walks, rocking from side to side on stumpy legs. Her tail circles like a helicopter rotor. We live right next to the train tracks, and she had to jump over them to enter our driveway.

"The Swiss frown!" I said to Daniele at dinner while wrapping my tagliatelle around my fork. "Maybe I said something wrong, but I'm positive I didn't."

"Tell me what you said," my husband said.

"The woman asked me how old Tootsie is. We've seen her in the neighborhood. Long black hair, sometimes in braids. Walks to the train station at one o'clock almost every day. My height. You've mentioned her strong perfume before."

"Stinkage." Daniele pronounces it like a fake French word.

"No. She smells nice."

"Tell me what you said."

"Tootsie ha sei ani."

Daniele started to laugh.

"Don't laugh at me. *'Ha sei ani.'*" I rolled all the words together, the way Italians do.

"It's *'anni'* —not *'ani.'*"

"Have you taught me that? I don't think you've taught me that."

"*'Anni'* is years. *'Ani'* is anuses. You told her that 'Tootsie has six assholes.'"

I scrunched up my lips and bent over to pick up my Tube of Fur, who was sitting next to my chair. A fog. I was living in a language fog. Tootsie tried to lick my nose.

"One 'n' is different than two," Daniele said. "*Anni.*"

"*Anni,*" I said, loudly.

"*Quanti anni hai*?" Daniele asked. Literally, in Italian, "How old are you?" is "How many years do you have?"

"*Ho quarantaquattro anni,*" I said, squishing all the words together and dragging out the "n's."

"*E quanti ani hai*?" Daniele asked. How many assholes do you have?

"*Solo uno.*" Only one.

"*Brava!*" My husband reached over and tapped my nose. "And this?" he asked. "How does this work?" ◆

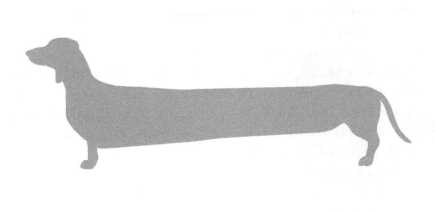

Free Tibet, Man!

DINTY W. MOORE

I drive all morning, fervent and focused on enlightenment, finally stopping for coffee at The Waffle House near Plain City, Ohio. My car sports a *Free Tibet* bumper sticker that I picked up in Atlanta, and as I lean against the left fender, sipping my cup of mindfulness, a young man spills out of a purple school bus and runs toward me. He is a 1990s version of a hippie—a white kid with dreadlocks, a knit cap, probably hemp, and Grateful Dead patches on his Levi's cutoffs.

"Hey, hey, free Tibet," he shouts, pointing to my bumper. "Free Tibet, man."

"Hey," I answer back.

"Free Tibet," he repeats. "Were you there?"

"Tibet?" I ask.

"No, man. The concert. Were you there?"

I realize he is talking about the Tibetan Freedom Concert in San Francisco, and that, to him, the grave situation in Tibet has mainly translated into an opportunity to hear the Red Hot Chili Peppers through really big speakers. I explain that I'm not primarily a music fan, but rather heading to Bloomington, Indiana, to see His Holiness the Dalai Lama.

The hippie kid tells me that he and his busload of pals are on their way to Woodstock, New York, for another music festival. "It's gonna be cool."

His girlfriend, a twenty-something, long-haired young woman in an oversize Mama Cass cotton dress and Birkenstocks, is on a pay phone about twenty feet away. She seems to be arguing with someone.

My new friend shouts to her:

"The Dalai Lama is in Bloomington. Wanna go?"

She waves and shouts back. "Free Tibet! I was there!!"

I give them a peace sign. There is nothing else to be done. ◆

The Tail End

AMY SHAW

I have a behind. Actually, I think it qualifies for the distinction of being called a badonkadonk. It's a family thing. You've got it if you favor the Sweet side. It is round, curvy, and really sticks out. Skinny girlfriends will ask where I got it. Standard answer is, "My mom," and that's the truth. Of all the traits and ticks found in our collective DNA, this one is by far the most annoying.

The bodacious backside. It gets noticed. It can be embarrassing. It is a lot of work. Since it is such a big deal, I have always been aware of the space it occupies. As a young girl, my nanna used to tap me on the derriere and say, "Love that tush." In college, between the big hair and how I filled out those harem pants, I was totally rockin' the "can't touch this" look. These days, I use my donk to dramatically emphasize common expressions such as "bringing up the rear", "bottoms up", or "sit on it". You know how it is; anything for a laugh.

How one feels about the patootie depends on the times. Right now, the J. Lo junk-in-the-trunk look is where it's at. My daughter and nieces shake their tail feathers about like prized possessions. Each day, the K. Kardashians exploit their moneymakers to maintain their celebrity status. Recording artists sing songs about the bonbon. Classics such as "Shake Your Bootie" and megahits like "All About That Bass" have us jiggling our fannies across the dance floor. Get this — if you think yours should be bigger, you can actually purchase enhancements, submit to injections, or even have plastic surgery to improve the bootiliciousness of your keister.

I, however, am a child of the '70s and '80s. White girls were supposed to be straight and flat. While Brooke was bragging nothing came between her and her Calvin's, I was struggling just to get the damn jeans over my caboose.

Then there is the apple bottom's nemesis—lines. Panty lines. You see, not only am I supposed to jam my salt shaker into the skinny jeans, but once I finally get them buttoned, I'm supposed to be able to flash a seamless, Queen Bey profile. Not quite there? No worries, dear—this is America, birthplace of inno-vation. We've got hosiery, the thong, and compression wear. One that snags and runs as soon as you leave your home; another that is referred to as butt floss and results in a perpetual wedgie; and, finally, a contemporary solution that pro-duces an oxygen-deprived blue hue throughout the body. Really, America—this is the best you could do?

If only I could loosen up and learn to embrace my wazoo. I could take advantage of a fat-bottomed girl's ability to make the rockin' world go round. I could sashay down the street, swing my hindquarters with moxie, and flash my "Oh yeah, this baby's got back" smile. I could post selfies of my backside and collect followers while I LMAO at the absurdity of it all. Most interestingly, I could wait until that evening when the earth and sun align, blast Van Morrison's jingle, and flash my full moon at whomever I like.

Sadly, I cannot be so carefree. As a female with a generous rumpus, all I really want is to be able to slip on my denims without bursting a blood vessel or breaking a nail. Mother Nature, however, has made up her mind and there is nothing a girl can do about this predicament. My fate has been cast. It is what it is. You can curse the gods, you can learn to love it, or you can squat, lunge, and sweat your gluteus maximus 'til you drop. It will not matter—it's here to stay—this anchor will not budge. In the end, it's best to enlist the strategies you use to deal with life's other annoyances. Because as each sun sets, the truth remains—it's simply a stubborn ass. ◆

Christmas Letter

RON CARLSON

Oh ho, another year has passed! Three hundred and sixty-five days, they say, though I've never counted—so many days! I counted once but it was like 7-8-9 and easy through January, which is coming our way like a rocket once again, but then I got to February 11-12-13, and what? How many days, let's just say it: hundreds! How to even measure them; the little devils slip by two at a time! Am I right? Enough days laid end to end to be a football field, that's right, with some to spare on each end, a tricky comparison but oh so true, and it helps us comprehend the magnitude of what has just transpired, is transpiring, with the fifty-two weeks, the little weeks, rushing by like traffic everybody on their cell phone, fifty-two, and there are fifty-two of everything. It's a common number and easy to get your head around, which sounds painful, right? Fifty-two cards in a deck which is perfect because some weeks are the six of clubs and some weeks are the jack of diamonds or the queen, and sometimes like the joker, which would make fifty-three weeks, but I do not care because they would all flee just as quickly, and I've never counted the weeks, how could a person remember every Monday, say, to count the week and file it away? Not going to happen. Even the months of this past year; I don't care how many there are, don't even say a number, as they are all gone, all forty or fifty of the months of this past year, gone and gone to where the years go and now there's a pile of them somewhere assuming they pile up like magazines on the coffee table somewhere far away, or maybe even very close, but still gone and not to be seen again, but what am I saying? Here's Christmas looking us in the face again; we remember this. The clock is ticking! Let's be happy now and now and now. The old year has gone. Here, take this gift. Let's raise a glass; what are we waiting for, Christmas? ◆

Sex and the Socratic Method

GINA BARRECA

"Use the Socratic method when having the birds-and-bees chat with your child," advised an earnest article recently published in a reputable magazine. "Ask your child 'When do you think is a good time to have sex?'"

I paused after I read this line.

I grew up in a cynical old-time Brooklyn household. The Socratic method, now that I think about it, was often employed in our family. The Socratic method was, I believe, instinctively passed down through our Sicilian family although it was slightly altered from the original Greek give-and-take method of discourse.

It was used not as a way to illuminate or encourage discussion, however, but instead as a way to drive home the severity of a person's error so they themselves could discover the depth of their transgression.

For example, you'd say to your sister who'd just set the table and put the food out for dinner, "Try this soup." You'd insist and she'd decline. Then you would say it again and again, insisting that she try the soup. Finally, she'd impatiently agree and ask, "Where's the spoon?" and you'd go "*Ah ha!*" in triumph because that was the point you were making the whole time. There was no spoon. She had neglected to give you appropriate cutlery.

The fact that you could reach the drawer where the cutlery was kept and get yourself your own lousy spoon without actually rising from your chair was not the point. She didn't set the table right. No spoon. She had to learn. It was Socratic method in action without being defined as such.

But nobody would have used it, or any other method, to discuss the birds and the bees.

First of all, talking about sex was not something anybody did.

Second of all, if you were going to talk about sex, which nobody did, you would never use the phrase "the birds and the bees." What are you, a gardener?

Third, if you did ask one of your offspring, "When do you think is a good time to have sex?" his answer would probably be, "Usually after the second cocktail," because you'd be having this conversation with your kid when he was twenty-seven, after he'd been married for six years and had four children of his own.

But haven't times changed? In 2014, does advice about having a straight-forward talk with your kids about sex still need to peek out coyly from behind a modesty curtain hung between John James Audubon (artist and ornithologist) and Burt Shavitz (who owned Burt's Bees before Clorox bought the company for $925 million a few years back)?

I attempted to pinpoint the first use of the phrase "the birds and the bees" as a euphemism for sex even before I finished reading the article. There are lots of theories: Some say it was a Cavalier poet; others claim it was Coleridge.

The most convincing argument is that the phrase was made widely popular through a publication put out by the eugenics movement around the turn of the last century. The collection, titled *Safe Counsel*, was reproduced many times in a short period of time (thereby ironically undermining the basis of the eugenic philosophy), and it included a description of a mama bird protecting her eggs and a father figure as a busy bee with pollen sticking to his hairy legs as he disseminates himself against flowers.

If the eugenics people wanted to keep folks out of the reproduction business, that description alone would do it.

Except that misinformation about sex is just about as pernicious as no infor-mation about sex. Both are worse than having lots of information about sex. The wised-up guys and girls never got into "trouble" because they knew what they were doing.

The poor souls whose families were too cowardly or whose schools were too constrained to teach them anything about sex were the ones most truly at risk.

It was my mother who told me about how children are conceived and how bodies worked. I've always been grateful to her, especially since anyone else in our family would have dropped their rosary beads at her honesty.

When is a good time to have sex? After you both understand what kind of decision you're making and fully accept the consequences.

And that's the right answer at any age. ◆

Argument with Myself on How to Write a Competent Essay

SCOTT LORING SANDERS

After fourteen years, the cherry tree has died. It was a gift from my wife, celebrating six months of sobriety. A kind gesture, one that always meant more to me than she knew. Every time I'd mow around it, I'd think about how I was still sober. Usually the thought only lasted a few seconds, though occasionally I'd get lost and reflect. On my last night as a hopeless drunk, I pounded twenty-eight beers. By myself. The tree lived fourteen years. Fourteen is half of twenty-eight, which . . .

Okay, seriously? Fourteen is half of twenty-eight? Cut everything except the first two lines.

What's wrong with it? I planned to explore how I struggled with alcohol for half my life.

Jesus, that's awful.

What do you mean? Too maudlin?

It's a prime example of a shallow writer trying to make ridiculous, nonexistent connections that are supposed to have some "deeper meaning, man." Lose the Zen or feng shui or whatever the hell, and just tell the story. And maudlin? Really? What an asshole-ish word.

I'm sad when I look at that dead tree now because it was a simple reminder of how my life had improved. But a disease invaded, which is fitting . . .

Let me guess. Alcoholism is a disease? It's hereditary? Every branch of your family tree has been touched by it; all your roots are soaked in alcohol?

Too cliché? Okay, how about this? I joked with my wife that maybe the tree's demise meant I could start drinking again. (Part of me wanted that to be true. Any excuse to drink, even after all this time, still lingers somewhere deep within.) To my surprise she said, "If you think you can handle it . . ." (Permission. It was an opening that my inner-demon—a demon who never quite died—pounced on immediately. What if? Maybe just one or two? It'd be nice to have a cold beer occasionally) ". . . but it's probably not worth chancing," she finished. And the little demon went dormant, stuffed back into its dark hole. Until the next test. So I plan to cut down the tree soon, burn it in the woodstove. It'll keep my family warm for a night . . . That's good, right? There must be a connection, some sort of ironic symbolism? Burning the devil who's haunted me or something?

Oh, puke. Is George Washington next? Can't chop down a cherry tree without giving him a shout-out.

Well, actually, the whole "never tell a lie" motif was a consideration. I mean, I lived a lie ever since that first drink—

You're really going there? Damn, we almost made it through this essay without that trite comparison. You hate authors who blatantly pull at your heart-strings. You want to punch them. Don't be a douchebag.

You know, I'm glad that word's back in the vernacular.

What word?

Douchebag.

On this we agree.

Remember as kids, in the late '70s? We used it constantly. Had no idea what it meant—and to this day, I've still never actually seen one—but man, what a word. Then it disappeared for thirty years. Now it's back.

Maybe douchebag is cyclical, like fashion.

Yeah, maybe. Remember when the vet advised, after the dog got sprayed by a skunk, that a douche was the best remedy?

Sure, but remind me again how that's remotely pertinent to this essay?

It's a cool aside.

Cut it. Your brain wanders when you write.

I'm keeping it.

Just tell the story.

I got sober. My wife bought a cherry tree to mark my six-month milestone. I was still foggy then, angry and bitter, struggling, but the gesture was kind. Fourteen years later, the tree has died, the leaves withered, the bark split and peeling like old paint. I pondered the significance, tried to impart some deeper meaning, but in reality it was just a dead tree. I don't need it to remind me of my progress. Every day is a reminder: no hangover, a clear world, life is great. Tomorrow I'll cut it down and burn it in the woodstove. When I feel that warmth, maybe I'll have a brief internal ceremony. Perhaps a second of reflection. Say, "Good job, dude," and that will be that. I'll go upstairs and watch college football. If I get real crazy, I might even crack open a ginger ale. Then I'll start a pot of chili or stew. Something hearty for a cold November evening. Mayb . . .

Stop. Less is more.

This?

Learn when something's finished.

It's only 750 words.

Precisely. ◆

The Long Pink Line

LISA ROMEO

"**A colonoscopy with no anesthesia**?" asks Dr. Kim. "In years, I never see this."

It's not you, it's me, my rigid control issues, my I-can-take-it, wimp-averse attitude. Mostly, my bottom-line desire to be conscious when a man with whom I am only slightly acquainted is about to insert a lubed-up thing into my nether regions.

That, and those words, *"even death,"* under "Complications–Rare" on the anesthesia consent form.

I ask Dr. Grossman, my calm, methodical gastroenterologist, who will be gazing into my entrails, if the anesthesia is for pain. *Because I pumped out two ten-pound kids without an epidural, get cavities filled without Novocain, and once, a horse used my foot for a footstool, and I had my big toenail extracted by an intern who left the lidocaine behind.*

"Because I have a high tolerance to pain."

"Without anesthesia, it's *uncomfortable,*" Dr. Grossman says evenly, like when he'd said my GI symptoms could be indigestion, ulcers, or cancer, and let's schedule a *little procedure.* "But it's safe to proceed without."

"I'm sure other people have done it."

Dr. Grossman nods. He is about seventy. "A few, over the years. We do pump in air and the probe goes around bends. At any point, Dr. Kim can have you asleep in seconds. Because it is *uncomfortable.*"

Nurse positions me on my side, twenty-four inches from a television monitor. She switches the set on, but says, "You should close your eyes."

And miss the show?

"Relax," Dr. Grossman says. I unclench my glutes, and the chilly lubed tube with attached microcamera begins its circuitous journey—a fantastic voyage. The tunneling trajectory angles upward, sideways, and I notice Nurse is rhythmically unspooling looped tubing like a backyard garden hose. I'm starting to feel as I do when I eat too many string cheeses, slightly *uncomfortable.* Just a ripple, a funky flutter.

"Doc, can you narrate?" I ask.

"You're *watching*?"

"Yes, it's fascinating."

The screen shows a fleshy undulating soft tube lined with spindly writh-ing reddish-pink spidery webs; a smooth subway excursion, slithering around bends; a shifting view of mauve specks, maroon spots, a mélange of cranberry blobs.

"Can you tell me what those structures are?"

"That? Stray fecal matter that didn't completely evacuate."

So I'm watching plops of poop when I realize I'm growing *quite uncomfort-able*. But coping.

"There's the problem," Dr. Grossman says, indicating something resembling a bulbous, swaying, stunted semi-erect penis. A polyp.

"We'll snip that out on the way back."

But now something is leaving concrete-filled balloons in its path.

"How you doing?" Dr. Grossman asks. I nod, since I can't chance speaking. He asks Nurse to feel my stomach.

"Still soft."

I'm thinking soft is good, relaxed. My navel is so far out in front of me I must resemble Octomom. I think I may combust.

"Still room," Nurse reports. Another air bong hit.

"You OK?" Dr. Grossman asks.

I sneak one final glimpse at the monitor and see only a glutinous, gross mess. I stare at the brass fittings on the doorjamb and remember a carpenter once describing a butt hinge. My body is growing, groaning. I can't imagine anything better than sticking a hatpin directly into my own abdomen.

"Yes, but it's . . ."

"Uncomfortable?" he asks, a little less Marcus Welby, more Sweeney Todd.

Dr. Grossman, I decide, needs a thesaurus. *Uncomfortable* is not synonymous with excruciating torture, harrowing agony, crushing misery. Uncomfortable, to me, is *annoying but tolerable, mild but endurable, incommodious but bearable.* Uncomfortable does not suggest the need for six Motrin, a heating pad, a quick painless death, or Mom.

Has Dr. Grossman noticed my hand gripping the table? My foot flexed in a way reserved for when moaning *yes*?

"One-third done. Farther than anyone else without anesthesia."

Are human abdomens designed to accommodate three basketballs, two grapefruit, and the Staples easy button?

"More air, Nurse," he orders.

I search for Dr. Kim. He is smiling, sort of.

"You want now?"

"Yes, yes," I moan, flailing to clutch his sleeve. But I grab the poor man's belt, pull him hard against the table. "I want."

And, I sleep.

Three years later, I need a second colonoscopy, and I smile when the anesthesiologist approaches. I try for small talk.

"Which type of anesthesia are you using?"

"Propofol. You know, the Michael Jackson drug," he says.

I want to say that the King of Pop, you know, *died* from that drug.

I nod and sign the waiver and extend my arm. ◆

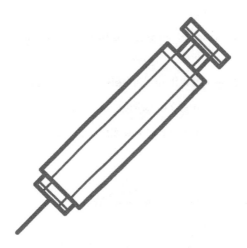

Bridge Metaphors Used During the Meeting with Department Heads

DOUGLASS BOURNE

- **You have to build bridges to other departments.**
- There isn't time to build bridges to other departments.
- Bridges build from two directions.
- We don't have the resources to be the only bridge builders.
- We've already built some bridges.
- How do you build a bridge when you have forty other projects going?
- At some point you can't just worry about the bridge, you have to think about the dock and ferries too.
- Before we build a bridge across, we have to secure the bridge to a strong foundation.
- Bridges can be cost-prohibitive. Tunnels might be better long-term investments.
- People are moving across the bridge in one direction.
- There have been bridges in place since the merger, and they are still in place.
- Sometimes bridges end in a silo.
- We need some large fish in the river. You need some perspective from the bridge.
- Do they just stop partway across the bridge?
- I had an experience where the bridge connected to a silo, and then it appeared there was a silo within a silo.

- Are there people on both sides of the bridge trying to get across?
- You can build bridges from each side but you have to make sure they meet in the right place.
- We don't have time to repair old bridges.
- Unless there is enough water, we might not even need a bridge. ◆

Life Among the Yankees

JULIANA GRAY

In my native South, Northerners (or Yankees, as we call them when we've had a little bourbon) are stereotyped as rude, loud, fast-talkers who'd just as soon spit on you as provide directions to Dunkin' Donuts. But after living in the North for nine years, I can report to my fellow Southrens that this stereotype is untrue. Most Yankees I know are polite, speak at a reasonable pace, and are glad to point you (loudly) toward the nearest cruller. However, I would like to share some other observations I've made about my Northern friends and neighbors.

I live in a small college town in western New York, which is not considered part of New England. The people here, many of whom are transplanted New Englanders, were very quick to tell me this. When they speak of New England, their eyes grow misty with emotion. The Boston Common! Apple cider! Fall foliage! A tender sob may escape their lips. At this point, if they are in any way descended from anyone who was ever aboard the *Mayflower*, saw the *Mayflower*, or caught a case of grippe whose viral strain evolved from those carried by rats aboard the *Mayflower*, they will let you know about it.

Upon meeting a Southerner, Yankees are very curious. "Is everyone really that racist?" they ask. "What *is* okra? Isn't it slimy? And are all Southerners racist?"

"Not everyone," I answer. "It's a seed pod. It's not slimy. Weren't you with me at Wegmans last week when we saw that truck with Confederate flag in the back?"

"Oh, but that truck had *Pennsylvania* plates," they respond.

In my Southern literature course, my Yankee students spend the first day brainstorming associations with the South. Most are negative—racism, rednecks, incest, and illiteracy top the list—but they're very polite about it. The positives are barbecue, fried chicken, peaches. Together we discuss their lists, and I push them to consider whether each item is specific to a geographical region, or whether they're more relevant to class, rural versus urban life, or economics.

Yes, they agree, we do have rednecks and racism in western New York. When we hit "accents," they balk. "I don't have an *ahyk*-cent!" they protest, honking like geese through their nasal cavities.

(If you want to hear a true western New York accent, try to steer the conversation toward the man-made waterway that flows through Rochester. "Oh, the Erie Can-*yahl*! I love going *kahy*-aking there!")

Yankees are a very earnest and optimistic people. I never thought of Southerners as particularly ironic until I lived among people who seem to think that Norman Rockwell, that sentimental Coke-shilling hack, was actually a Walker Evans-esque documentarian. Yet they mean well. I know a man who donated one of his kidneys, not to any particular recipient, but because it was a truly benevolent thing to do. Yet when that man went skiing the next day, I knew he was just showing off.

Once, I was crossing a strip mall parking lot; it was fall, and an icy wind whipped the shoppers' scarves around their necks like garrotes. A woman cupped her hands around her mouth and bellowed to another woman several rows away. "Nicole! NIH-COOOOOOLE! I got apple butter for you!"

That utterance, with its aggressive enthusiasm for sharing the bounty of the autumn harvest, is the most Yankee sentence I've ever heard. Here are some more Yankee sentences I've jotted down over the years:

"I've always wanted to see the Saint Lawrence Seaway."

"We could kayak to the farmer's market!"

"I also need to pick up some lingonberry preserves, if you have any recommendations."

"Oh, we should make maple creamies!" (*Note*: I have no idea what a maple creamy is. I suspect it is either a candy, or a seasonal sex act invented by Robert Frost. Either way, the woman who spoke the above sentence was really into it.)

Here are some more quick facts about Yankees: They all have allergies. The women can wear up to six scarves at a time. It is mandatory that they wear at least one scarf at all times. If you complain about the winter weather, they will suggest that you take up skiing, as if *more* exposure to winter weather is the solution. "Cross-country skiing is just like running!" they will lie to your face.

If any of my Yankee friends read these notes, they will object, but they'll be very polite about it. ◆

Inner Nonna

TERRI FAVRO

She appeared unexpectedly about five years ago: my Nonna Rosa, born in Piacenza,1894; emigrated to New York City, New York, 1911; steamed back to Italy, 1920; floated back to New York City, 1926; deported to Canada, same year. I've been seeing a lot of her lately. Thing is, she's been dead for over thirty years. But every time I glance in the mirror there she is, looking back at me, as though she's had a hard night of novenas. Despite spinning classes and nature-defying hair color, my genes have spoken: I'm turning into my grandmother, a turn-of-the-last-century Italian woman whose style sense ran to clean aprons and scapular medals.

It's not that I didn't love her; I just never expected to *be* her. Being Canadian born, I aspired to grow up into one of those "matching purse and shoes" ladies—the kind who throw cocktail parties, use a cigarette holder, and have affairs with the pool boy. (Not that anyone in my neighborhood ever *had* a pool boy—it's just that I saw *Valley of the Dolls* at an impressionable age.)

From childhood, I felt I was destined to become a Lauren Bacall or an Eva Gabor: bony blondes tossing back martinis and tossing out snappy one-liners. But by my forties, my innate Nonna-ness started asserting itself. The less-than-amusing laugh lines. The hollowing of the cheeks, giving me that saintly martyr look. The facial hair. There are some legacies that even a good wax product won't strip away.

It's probably not surprising that Nonna went for men who were spiritually and physically muscular (and not necessarily in that order). She was devoted to Saint Francis of Assisi and Saint Anthony of Padua, but also enjoyed ogling stripped-to-the-waist TV wrestlers on Channel 11's Saturday Afternoon Wrestling. Nonna's champion was The Beast, an immense, hairy man whose ring persona was a barely civilized über-male, a sort of Canadian version of Enkidu, who would leap into the ring and try to pound the shit out of the good guys in a most unsportsmanlike manner. The Beast wrestled to be hated: Nonna loved him, or at least was intrigued by his strange animal charms. "*Guarda, guarda, Teresina!* He looks like he came out of the bush," she'd tell me again and again, shaking her head with a little smile while she sat two feet from the screen, squinting at the flickering black-and-white images of large men doing flying dropkicks. Meanwhile, Nonno would be smoking cigars with his drinking buddies at the Polish Veterans Legion or hiding in the garden, throwing his profanities at the weeds. He always made himself scarce when the wrestling was on, like it was some kind of woman's thing.

It turned out that The Beast was actually a French-Canadian family man named Yvon Cormier, according to the loving obituary he received in Toronto's *Globe and Mail*. I'm glad Nonna didn't live long enough to read it, as the truth about The Beast's gentle nature would have punctured her dreams.

Other people's grandmothers, I've since learned, took their grandchildren to *The Nutcracker* or professional children's theater, or perhaps a puppet show. Nonna Rosa took me to see the professional midget wrestlers at Garden City Arena. Their diminutive size made them acceptable for a girl my age to watch, as they threw one another to the mats and into the ropes, sweating mightily from their tiny, but extremely well developed, pecs and biceps.

"*Guarda, guarda*, Teresina, look at their little shoes!" Nonna would enthuse, pointing out the tiny slippers they left in the corner while they fought with the ferocity of very small men.

Despite this affection for wrestlers, large and small, Nonno remained quite passionate about my grandfather until the end of her life. She confided to me once, with a look that was, I think, supposed to indicate Nonno's own hidden beastlike qualities: "Nonno may be a good man now, but not when he was young." And then she went misty-eyed and added, sotto voce, "But he was the best-looking man in the village."

The science is irrefutable: the genes I inherited from Nonna Rosa made me a pushover for Saints Anthony and Francis (Bennett and Sinatra, respectively, in my case), and for handsome men with hard muscles and heads to match. When it comes to aprons and scapular medals, the hell with science. Shake me a martini. ◆

Gadget Graveyard

LIANE KUPFERBERG CARTER

There's a graveyard in my basement.

The lower level of my house is the final resting place for dead and discarded kitchen appliances: those innovative, time-saving, cunning devices you buy in a flurry of anticipation and eagerness, convinced they'll transform you into a domestic goddess.

My basement shelves are stacked with gimmicky gadgets that no longer work, never worked, or never even made it out of their boxes. In my defense, many of these items were gifts. But if you want to chart three decades of culinary trends, well hey, *come on down!*

I present you the forensic evidence: the Zojirushi bread machine. The fondue set. The panini press. The pasta maker. The Crock-Pot, s'more set, smoothie shaker, Salton hot tray, Big City Slider Station, yogurt kit, electric carving knife, George Foreman grill, ice cream maker, food vacuum sealer, wine aerator, Bialetti espresso pot, coffee bean burr grinder, Excalibur food dehydrator (to make—what? beef jerky?), and three—count 'em, three—cappuccino machines.

Best of all?

The blow torch for caramelizing crème brûlée.

"Who's going to use that?" my husband demanded.

"I will," I lied.

But wait! There's more! as Ron Popeil used to say. You remember Ron, king of the infomercial. He gave us the Veg-o-Matic, the Inside-the-Shell Egg Scrambler, the Showtime Rotisserie, and the immortal phrase, "Set it and forget it!" You know his gadgets. The ones that *Slice!* And *dice!* And have *a million and one uses!* The cuter the name, the less functional.

Yet even my sensible husband has fallen prey to a manic sales pitch. "I bought Ginsu knives," he confesses.

I console him. "No worries. I ordered a Salad Chopper."

Bought with such zeal and high hopes, only to be consigned months later to the abyss of our windowless basement. Why did I succumb? What inner *kitchenista* was I channeling? Betty White in her role as Happy Homemaker Sue Ann Nivens? A Top Chef? Did I see myself as a braless earth mother in Birkenstocks, baking sheets of cookies to serve with milk from the cow in the backyard? Or as Nigella Lawson, stirring up sensual, simmering reduction sauces?

Kitchen gadgets have sex appeal. They're all shiny and new. You think they'll change your life, and of course they rarely do (though I still swear by my Cuisinart Smart Stick immersion hand blender.) They're just countertop candy. More affordable that a midlife Ferrari, but in the end? Kitchen porn that teases but doesn't deliver.

Because, really: What's the sense in having a gadget that chops everything in half a minute, when you then have to spend the next twenty disassembling, hand-washing, and reassembling it?

Last night we finally hauled out the never-used panini press still in its original packaging and checked the directions. "Practical hints: it is recommended to adapt cooking according to your own taste." Duh. It also advised, "Apply a thin coat of oil to the heating plates." To a nonstick grill? But oil it I did. That sucker really heated up. It was smoking. Made pretty nifty grill marks too. It took five minutes to eat our fancy sandwiches, and four hours before the thing cooled down enough to clean.

"It would be a heck of a lot easier to clean if they'd designed it to remove the grill plates," my husband grumbled. "How are you supposed to get rid of the soap when it says you can't submerge the unit? I've been over this thing with a wet rag three times!"

"How do restaurants clean their grills?"

"They don't."

"Maybe it's like a wok?"

"It doesn't get that hot."

"Au contraire." I offered my blistered finger as evidence.

"Wouldn't it be easier to toast the sandwiches next time?" he asked.

Back to the basement. Rest in peace, panini press. We hardly knew ye. ◆

It's Not Always Easy Being a Man

NICK HOPPE

I was in a bad mood, and had been for a couple of days. No reason. Business was fine, family was fine, health was fine. I was just in a bad mood and wanted to show the world, starting with my wife.

It took her three days to notice, but she finally realized my one-word responses and sullen attitude were a bit out of the ordinary.

"What's the matter?" she asked. "Something wrong?"

"Everything's fine," I replied, squaring my manly shoulders. "I'm just having my period."

Like most women, she didn't take kindly to me attacking their territory, but I didn't care. I tell it like it is, and I had no other reason to be in a bad mood.

"Hey, I've got hormones, too," I said as she tried to wave me off. "And let me tell you—they're raging right now."

"Men don't get periods," she replied. "I don't know where you get these ideas."

"Well, I've got news for you, little lady," I huffed. "For your information, I've got . . . IMS!!!!"

She actually looked at me with curiosity, which I took as a victory. "What the hell is IMS?"

"Irritable Male Syndrome," I confidently answered. "I read all about it in Cosmopolitan."

I could have predicted her response. "First of all, what are you doing reading Cosmopolitan? And second, you're out of your mind."

"Yes, I am a little out of my mind, but that's because I happen to have IMS right now. I chart these things. You'll be happy to know I don't get it every month. More like every ten weeks."

I actually don't chart it, but when you have IMS you don't really care about exaggerating. It just seems like every ten weeks or so, so I went with it.

"What about menopause?" she asked, looking for ways to defuse my condition. "Shouldn't you be too old to be getting your period?"

I wasn't deterred. In fact, I was encouraged. "Maybe that explains the hot flashes I've been getting lately. Do you think there's some light at the end of the tunnel for my IMS episodes?"

She actually patted me on the shoulder. "That's why they call it the Golden Years."

My mood actually brightened with the news. I could actually see a time, far in the future, when my hormones would no longer fluctuate wildly, and I could blame a bad mood on something that actually happened in my life.

The discussion ended, though, and we went to bed without her being convinced I was having my period. So when I woke up with night sweats, I let her know.

"Oh, my God," she said sleepily. "It's just hot in here. Open a window."

She just didn't get it. Women never do. Irritated, I got up the next morning and went right to the computer and printed out the Cosmopolitan article about Irritable Male Syndrome.

She skimmed it while eating breakfast, but she couldn't miss the part I circled. It asked the question, "What should you do when he's male PMS-ing?"

She read the answer aloud. "Talk to your man if his moodiness becomes an issue. If you think your guy is on his 'period' or experiencing some IMS, cut him some slack."

I nodded from across the table as she read. Maybe now that Cosmopolitan had investigated the issue, she would understand what I was going through.

Or maybe not. Apparently, Cosmopolitan is a step below the New England Journal of Medicine when it comes to diagnosing bodily health.

"OK, I'll cut you some slack," she said. "I will admit that you are in a bad mood for no reason whatsoever, and that your testosterone level must have dropped considerably."

I didn't like her tone. "What do you mean by that?" I asked, worried where this was going. "I'm talking about my mood, not my manhood."

"You said your hormones were off, and I'm agreeing," she answered, tossing the article to the side. "I'm cutting you some slack and being sympathetic."

Smart woman. Very smart woman. My unexplained bad mood went away, never to be discussed again. ◆

Jobs, A to Z

JENNY KLION

Dear Human Resources,
Your assistant mentioned you were having trouble placing me, so I've enclosed a revised resume, alphabetized, mostly, for your convenience.

Thanks for taking a closer look.

Best,

Jenny Klion

- I was an Apprentice for the Pickle Family Circus in San Francisco, a long time ago.

- Also, a Barista at a comedy club in San Francisco, before Barista was a thing. I'm always there before something is a thing. I even flirted with that old *SNL*-er Rob Schneider there, before he was a thing.

- I've been a Comedian, a Circus Clown, and a Cook on a fishing boat. Plus, Copy Editor for a variety of smut houses—because grammar is very important in pornography.

- I was a Dental Assistant, for one day. Also, a Dishwasher at an Italian restaurant when I was seventeen, which was so Disgusting I left to be that Cook on a fishing boat.

- I've been an Essay Writer, and an Emcee at a performance art club, before that was a thing. But also a French Fry Cook at a Hard Rock Cafe, where I first started to question the nature of my existence.

- I've been a Grant Getter and Game Show Writer, plus a Hollywood Studio Executive for Jim Henson Pictures, during which time my beautiful daughter was born.

- I Interviewed Dick King Smith, of *Babe* fame, in case anybody remembers that sweet pig movie, for a Scholastic magazine.

- Also, a Juggler, and my personal favorite, Jewelry Finder. This means I found jewelry and gems everywhere, and turned *that* into a business.

- K: Maybe I'm a Kiss Ass. As for L, I'm a Letter Writer, both professional and otherwise. See the *New York Times, New York Daily News,* and the bottom of my desk drawer.

- I was also a bad Magician for a while, when I was that Emcee that one time, before *that* was a thing.

- I've had a Newspaper Column, and was a Natural Foods Breakfast Cook at a theater school in the middle of Nowhere, Wisconsin. I was also an Opera singer in Edinburgh, playing Mrs. Rockefeller, which demonstrates I know how to hang with the big boys.

- I work in Publishing, as a Proofreader, and have Performed as a Puppeteer, with Big Apple Circus, among others. You can actually see part of my shadow-Puppet act in Woody Allen's movie *Alice,* which was way before *he* had a thing.

■ I've nearly been a Quadriplegic, but not exactly, though I once had to spend over four weeks in the Spinal Cord Injury Rehab Center at Mount Sinai Hospital. This wasn't a job per se, but it seemed like it was.

■ I've been a Receptionist, and still work as a Reader of book manuscripts and film lit, a thankless job, no matter how many times I am Right. I was also on the Rigging Crew for Philippe Petit, when he walked a high wire across the constellations at the top of Grand Central Terminal.

■ I was a Sax player, at the Palace of Fine Arts in San Francisco, as well as a Scallop Shucker, Sandwich Maker, Sauté Cook, Short Order Cook, plus a Script Adaptor, Script Consultant, Seamstress, and Substitute Teacher.

■ Also, a Trout Cook at a restaurant designed by Frank Lloyd Wright in Spring Green, Wisconsin, and once I worked one half of one day at a Taco Bell in Santa Cruz, California. You had to wear that horrible uniform, clean the counters every five seconds, and when my then-crush walked through the front door, I left on my lunch break and never went back.

■ I've been an Understudy, an Underground Bakery Owner, and an Unemployment Receiver.

■ V is for Violin, but no, I never did that. I never ran a Victory Lap either. Though maybe in that rehab center, when I could walk again after I couldn't. Further information upon request.

■ I've been a Waitress, and a Wire Walker myself, but don't get too excited— the cables were crotch-level only.

■ W is also for Writer, Writer's Assistant, and Wishing I'd gotten the credit I deserved on that Tony-nominated musical, and that celebrity chef memoir.

■ I've been an Xtra on a number of movie sets, including for Spike Lee and Eddie Murphy, and even twerked in the house of a Run DMC video, before that was a thing.

■ Young Playwrights, NYC, hired me for my first script-reading job.

■ And Z, no, nothing Z. I'm a lot of hot air actually. Though Zachary Zembobber was the name of my daughter's first—and last—boyfriend. ◆

Hard-On

SVEN BIRKERTS

"Hard-on." What a vexation. I don't mean the Kantian thing-in-itself, but the word. Or is it a phrase? I'm trying to remember how old I was when it first confused me. I'm pretty sure it was after grade school, certainly long after we'd all been saying "boner" and "rod," the two words which for a long time divided the world between them. Anyway, at some point 'hard-on' started showing up in our bus-stop deliberations, bringing with it great uncertainty. There was, for starters, the period when I had it wrong, when I thought that when some kid said that so-and-so gave him a hard-on, he was saying "*heart* on." I thought it was a metaphor: He was in love. And I wondered, for I was a linguistic precisionist even back then, where such an odd image might have originated. Was it some kind of regional kenning, like when old sailors called the ocean "the whale road"? How nice. "Don't tell anyone, but I have a heart-on for Ginny." I'm thinking now that it's good that I've never been inclined to offer such confidences to others. And what a mortification it was then to find out that I'd been wrong—not just in hearing, but in my attribution of meaning. *Hard-on*, you idiot! What a comedown, what an education. The plummet from sacred to profane, from that benign decal to—to what, exactly? Again, the language obscured more than it revealed. I cracked my young teen brain over it. Hard-on, hard-on . . . Now that I was older, I got the "hard" part. But why "on"? *On what?* Language was a meaning system, and words had but one purpose: to signify. If it was not a "hard" but a "hard-on," then there had to be a reason. I worked at it like Houdini addressing a knot. *On.* Well, "on" was usually used as a preposition; it did not, pardon me, dangle. If "on" was used prepositionally, it generally preceded a noun. "Ginny put the book *on* the table." But when I thought about "hard-on" and what I now knew It to refer to, I was at a loss. Though not having had the real experience for which it was a biological prerequisite, I somehow knew that the point of the business was not the laying of the said hard thing *atop*, but its insertion *in*. In which case, why not "hard-in"? Though that didn't sound quite right either. There was the other component, the "hard." It felt wrong to conjoin an adjective with a preposition and then just let them stand. I worked and worked. The only visualization that made any sense—and not that much of it—was of the item in question lying upon the stomach—one's own or that of another (though the latter imagining was almost as inconceivable as that where it was actually *in* somewhere . . .). But here the logician raised his querulous head, objecting that if "hard" were to have meaning here then its referent could not be honorably said to lie upon anything—verticality and proneness being in essential opposition. I exhausted myself in conjuring, never once considering that *on* could here be a contraction—of the word "one," say. But even that, as I think of it now, poses certain problems. The familiar contraction for "one" is *un*, as in, "He's a fine young-un." And I have never heard anyone say "hard-un." No, it's always "hard-on," square and solid. What's more, even supposing the word is, etymologically, such a contraction—calling it a "hard one" feels off. "Hard won," maybe, but that's a whole other bit of business. My ear is troubled by saying. "I have a hard one." It hints that there might be others. As in, "I also have a not-so-hard one." As if I keep a whole collection. Also, that makes it sound like a thing apart, a possession, something one *has*, or *owns*. We don't usually distinguish our body parts through claims of ownership. "I have a head, I have a foot." Well, of course I do. "I have a sore stomach." OK, that makes more sense. But a stomach is a stomach, and the adjective describes it. What is a "one"? Is it a stretch to say, looking from on high, that what most readily comes to mind is the Arabic numeral? It is. But who cares? If I did at the outset, I do no longer. It serves only to illustrate one of the many conturbations of my younger years. ◆

The Dachshund Endures

ROBIN HEMLEY

Every day, I picked up Milo, my miniature dachshund, and brought him to the patio, where I pressed on his bloated bladder and a strong string of pee arced out. Holding him aloft like a communion chalice, I pressed firmly, directing his pee wherever I wanted. On cold days, on rainy days, on hot days, I did this with him several times a day. Sometimes I wrote in his pee on the patio cement. Milo always stayed completely still as I did this, his paws drooping slightly, motionless. My wife had expressed him, too, though it was more often my job. Take out the recycling. Express Milo. Odd, he never had any particular mien I could discern as I did this. If you expressed me—of course, you'd need to be a giant as I stand 6 feet and weigh 87 kilos—holding me naked while squeezing my bladder, I would squirm, I would scream. I would be mystified. My penis would retract. Milo's penis was that special alarmed red of dog penises.

Milo endured, his eyes round and wide, but not out of fear, I thought. Sometimes, his right leg trembled, but it did this at other seemingly innocuous times, too. Once, while I sat at the kitchen table paying bills, I glanced at Milo dragging his hind legs. He stopped at his water dish and drank, and the muscles of his right leg twitched, as though some race were being run directly beneath the skin. When he was finished, he gave me a look (*Do I know you?*) and started the journey back to his bed in the living room. Milo stopped midway, trying to turn his head to see what was going on, as poop emerged with locomotive force from his butt. (*Does that belong to anybody?*)

Milo's malady is not uncommon among dachshunds, something I wish I'd known when I bought him foolishly and impulsively at a pet store after another dog of mine suddenly died. I didn't know what I was getting into—that Milo would slip a disc when he was five, and that as a result I would have to express him several times a day.

When my first wife and I divorced, she left the state with our children, Olivia and Isabel, shedding Milo, a final, parting gift to me. Either that, she said, or

he'd have to be put down. I couldn't have that on my conscience, so I took pee-
ing, pooping Milo, plus a closet filled with thousands of catalogs and maybe a
hundred cardboard boxes from a shopping channel. It took a wheelbarrow and
many trips to get rid of those catalogs.

Many days, I bemoaned my fate, not his. How could I have been reduced
to this, squeezing a dachshund's bladder several times a day? I used to be a
grown man with a marriage, a mortgage, children, but it was I who felt somehow reduced to Milo's size, I who felt keenly life's many indignities, when it
should have been Milo. But it wasn't. Milo endured. I don't know what went on
in that miniature brain of his. Not much, I'm sure. To Milo, life was life, pride
and indignity irrelevant. We did not understand each other, but we shared these
moments nonetheless, both of us single-minded, waiting for something to be
finished, and for that pleasant emptiness afterward. ◆

Playing the Chicken

MEG POKRASS

The acting teacher, Dante, has cast me as a chicken in the final yearly production. This makes me feel lumpy, short, and invisible. Playing a chicken feels like being disliked.

He casts blonde, giggly Melinda for the leading role. The kids he casts for the better roles are the ones who squeal when he walks into class—and they all happen to have light hair. I have dark hair and a curved nose.

Melinda is the most motivated. She has started jumping up and grabbing his ponytail, thrusting out her nonexistent tits and narrowing her pool-blue eyes.

I try to hide my disappointment but I feel myself sulking.

"This character is not just a chicken," Dante says. "It is a counterintuitive symbol of hope."

When acting class first started, I loved Dante. He was nice to me. He'd lift me up and plop me down and lift me up again because I was so light.

But, these days, he'll ask how my big sister's film-acting career is going and I don't understand the details he wants. He'll ask for the name of her agent, and I'll shrug—feeling my face redden.

"Tell her I'm her biggest fan," Dante says.

My sister says I should not have to play a chicken at all—and that even though pink feathers may look attractive on me and bring out my skin tone, it is ultimately unfair.

"Symbol of hope, my ass," my sister says. She tells me to stand up to Dante, to refuse.

At the first read-through, I tell Dante that my sister says hi to him, and that she thinks I should play a human, even if the human is a village idiot or a gnome.

He says, "I'll tell you what. Invite her here to watch the next rehearsal, and we'll figure something out together. Maybe she'll teach us some stuff."

When I ask her, she says, "No fucking way, this is bribery."

I love it when she says fuck. She says it often and I like to sing it in my head. Last year I was kicked out of Girl Scouts for saying that perfect word.

I keep imagining how and when I will say it to Dante. And, I remind my sister that a chicken has a past and lots of motivation. I test to see if it will soften her stance. I tell my sister that it will be a fun challenge, even though I really don't think so.

She says, "Of course. And you'll do great. But, fuck him anyway."

Mom doesn't notice anything, as usual. She's working three jobs now and can't be bothered. She does not sleep and she hates the world for warming up, hates it for all of its crazy-assed problems. She doesn't seem to think that me being cast as a chicken is good, bad, or worth worrying about. I believe she is right. Anyway, I'm telling myself that I will be a marvelous chicken. ◆

Boy Leaves Connecticut for New York, Becomes Nervous

SAM FERRIGNO

In the middle of February, I got a new job and a new apartment in New York. Had I anywhere near the amount of control over my life that I desired, I wouldn't have timed these things to occur in the same week. In February. What all began with excitement and bravos, took a sharp dive into stress and exhaustion, which somehow mutated into a blood infection. That is at least what three doctors guessed based on the enlarged size of my spleen and black tonsils. Not in twenty-five years of living had I seen doctors lose his poker face the way they did while shining a light into the back of my throat.

"Oh my god!" One of them said. "Have you *seen* this?" His face went from natural shock to the kind of glee that only a scientist can garner from human decay.

"Yes," I said, worried I had been selected by nature to model the rare and deadly effects of leaving one's cushy, Connecticut hometown for a city where the sun is blotted out by tall buildings. We would never know the cause, however, since my test results for mono, strep, gonorrhea, HIV, and herpes (why not?) came back negative. The failing of my body at this pivotal time, a time when it needed to run at top speed, was a mystery. Maybe I hadn't been broken in for adulthood yet, and this move was a sort of maturation baptism.

"You're just overtired," my mom said on the phone while I blew up an air mattress in my new, Tupperware-size bedroom. I was relieved. I love it when people say I look tired. I always want to say back, "Yes! I *am* tired, and I should really lie down for the rest of the day like a cat, don't you think?" Except this time, I didn't have to fake it by sighing or pressing two fingers into the bridge of my nose. I really was exhausted. Days after I trained someone to take over my old job, my new job would begin. The memory of exiting one office and the imagined trial-by-fire to come was enough to make my eyes cross before noon.

As I said goodbye to mom, I stopped blowing up my "bed" and laid down. To my astonishment, it fit without bending in half—there was no space between it and three of the walls, but it fit it did. A far cry from my old room in Connecticut, which accommodated people *and* furniture.

I glanced around my new chamber, my all-white, high-ceilinged cell. I marveled at how my first paycheck would only cover about 90% of one rent check for this place. Possibly out of dependency issues, I began to imagine New York as a tough-love maternal figure. One that would say, "You want comfort? Earn it, my little cretan." Its actual voice of car horns, shouting, and the occasional discharging of a firearm were omnipresent. New York is like a wealthy parent that is at once overbearing and negligent. Everything is close up, as if people with no sense of personal space created it, and yet in a distant cloud; miles (or perhaps inches) from your shoulder there is the notion that all it wants is your money, that you are one buck-wild spending spree from apologizing to strangers for money. That is, of course, absurd: Anyone browsing sensible springtime scarves at Urban Outfitters is not on the brink of homelessness—the brink of popcorn for dinner, maybe.

A professor boasted to me once that she was a "hooker at heart," meaning she eagerly took speaking, writing, and editing jobs if it meant bringing home some dough for herself or for a women's health charity she founded. Since I had only the one sub-poverty-line paying job and no charities to speak of, I thought, maybe I'll just be a hooker at 36th and 10th and see how that goes. Prostitution's been trending for centuries, right?

I knew deep in my engorged spleen that I was only scared because I had crash-landed onto a new plane of reality—one where comfort was earned and not given, which isn't a bad thing. No one ever rode a bike by pretending to balance. In an almost-prayer, I said to myself, "No matter what, faking it is not acceptable." Depending on how things go, that'll either be my life motto, or my sales handle on Craigslist. ◆

1-800-UHOH

R. C. VAN HORN

It was possible that my third chakra was blocked. No, my second. Perhaps I should have looked at my root. My crown was all fucked. Yes, my crown was fucked. I would never reach enlightenment with a fucked crown. And my chi was wonky. My chi was definitely wonky. I felt it. There was also a block in my liver, which houses anger. I felt anger. It was directed at my father, maybe. Or maybe my mother. Or maybe myself. How could I follow my North Star if my chi and my crown were guiding me toward the underworld? It was making my aura muddy. I needed to cleanse. Maybe with yoga and meditation and crystals and incense and astrology and the Enneagram and brain imaging and visualization and journaling and tapping. These I would do, possibly all at once, possibly in the waxing crescent moon, for I was a self-help junky.

People don't come to self-help lightly. They're tired. They're sick. They've tried therapy, or perhaps they don't believe in it. They might have mental illness or maybe they're just a little funny in the upstairs. We're all a little funny in the upstairs, really. I could go off about society, a long *Into the Wild*-like lecture that leaves me on my knees, but I won't. I'll just say this: I was a little funny in the upstairs. Rather, I was desperate.

Imagine this: you're eighteen years old and know beyond anything in the world that you must find your spirit animal. You must find your spirit animal because it will guide you to your inner wisdom, which will lead you to your career, your boyfriend, a closer family, and potentially a good sandwich. You know that you are a wolf, but you have very few wolf-like qualities. You are an aspirational wolf. You are more like a lemming, and this makes you sad. Realizing that you are a lemming has the capacity to sink you into a depression for days. You decide that you must consult the wolves.

Dear Wolves:

I am eighteen years old and afraid of human beings. Recently I was taking a test in Environmental Studies 101 writing an eloquent dissertation on the rising rates of estrogen levels in fish, which I loved, was obsessed with, but halfway through the exam I couldn't remember a damn thing. My mind was blank. This happens sometimes: when I am in groups, really anytime there's more than one person; in elevators; the threat of snakes (i.e., menacing-looking string or lace), having too much to shovel; talking to authority figures with fancy neckwear; those sorts of things. I watched as my classmates filed out of the room, as if they were wizards, and felt like the lemming I knew myself to be.

My professor said I could finish the exam in the library if I went to therapy. He was wearing a bow tie. My dumb eyes just peered up at him blankly, as if I was a little fish with too much estrogen.

A few days later I found myself sitting in the college counseling center, which is how I met Destiny. It was clear that Destiny and I weren't quite the right fit. I knew this because I was the equivalent of an eighteen-year-old repressed fundamentalist drill sergeant and she was like a drugged-out moon leader from a California desert community. We weren't quite on the same page. I needed a little help, sure, but I feel like I have to do this myself, at my own pace.

Would you be my guide?

Thanks.

Once I started speaking to the wolves it was only a matter of time until I joined a cult. It turned out that I was highly susceptible. Did I say one? Ha. I meant three. It was cult-light, just the outer reaches. I *barely* joined and they were *barely* cults. And all those energy healing podcasts I was listening to, and subsequently purchasing their products? Well, it was basically the cost of a copay, right? Just a lot of copays.

Now I'm proud to say that I've got my head squarely rooted on my shoulders. I know that I'm not a wolf, or a lemming. I mean, jeez. I'm obviously a Northern-Saw-Whet-Owl-NFJ-four-wing-five-Enneagram-Scorpio-(Libra cusp). How could I have been so misled? Anyway, thanks for the help, wolves. ◆

How I Ended Up Nearly Bald

DIANE PAYNE

The hairdresser was listening to Christian music, singing along quietly. She smelled like a pack-a-day smoker, which gave her voice that gravelly gruffness. The hope that Arkansas could become a wet state if a bill passed on Election Day almost made me giddy, probably the same way Heaven made the hairdresser giddy. To make small talk, I told her how great it'd be if we could buy beer at the grocery store, not the liquor store miles away out of town.

The hairdresser looked at me through the mirror, wanting to make sure I was paying attention to her face while she spoke. "Well, I guess if people are going to drink, they're going to buy it somewhere." She took a large chunk of my hair, looked directly into the mirror to make sure I noticed, and chopped it off.

Pray for redemption la da da. The music only fueled me. I refused to switch topics.

She seemed to know the exact miles to the nearest liquor store outside of our county. Why couldn't she own up to buying a six-pack? The redemption music continued playing, and I continued talking about how my life would improve if I could buy my beer while getting my groceries. She held up another huge chunk of hair, gave me that same testy look, and lopped it off. This was not a little trim. She was going for a crew cut.

"We could probably have a great city pool with all the tax money from alcohol," I said, trying to make the conversation more upbeat. I wondered if she was Pentecostal, one of those folks who don't believe in bathing suits either, because the next chunks of hair were lopped off rather quickly.

Avoid sinners, la da da . . .

When my daughter was an infant and I was weary of men hitting on me, I urged a hairstylist to keep cutting my hair, though he kept begging to me to reconsider. "More," I demanded over and over, and he shook his head and sighed sadly.

I didn't want to end up with that crew cut again, so I asked her something about her mother, who gave birth to nine kids and whose husband never let her mom learn to drive. I figured her dad was a drunk bastard and my hair was going to pay the price for his drunken brawls. I let out a sigh of relief when she told me he was dead, and just cut a small chunk of my hair.

"Ah, good," I said, hoping she'd think I liked my haircut now, and that I was glad her dad was six feet under.

"He was a damn drunk. Excuse my language," she said. "Let me even it out just a bit more."

My hair took one more loss for the drunks.

She gloated a bit as she turned my chair around, lifted the mirror, and then asked, "What do you think?"

I shook my head like a wet dog, and said, "It's time for a beer."

I left my fifteen bucks on the counter, listened to her sing one more chorus of some song where she kept repeating, "All you need is Jesus, la da la."

All I needed was beer and a bit more hair, la da la. ◆

Popcorn for Ling-Ling Nguyen

THOMAS JEFFREY VASSEUR

One afternoon in study hall for overachievers, misfits, and "class clowns," our point guard, Alan Poindexter, and I hatched a plan to break the monotony and hopefully impress our female fellow inmates. Two cheerleaders were arguing about lip gloss and plucking their eyebrows. Overseer and trigonometry teacher, Ms. Johnson, was engrossed in *Wuthering Heights,* which had been preceded by *Middlemarch,* and before that *The Hound of the Baskervilles.* Only valedictorian-to-be Elizabeth Reed, and transfer student Ling-Ling Nguyen, stuck with their equations.

While walking toward our cafeteria—the place reeked of onion salt and I'd come in second place for senior class president on a promise to "Abolish Taco Casserole"—Alan had gotten a taste of Ling-Ling's beautiful laughter. He'd also heard her tell Beth Reed that she absolutely adored popcorn, the impetus being the industrial-size chrome popper used for home games in the adjacent gymnasium.

"We'll just ask for bathroom permission," he whispered, "then fire it up."

"What about Coach Vannerson? If he catches us, we're toast."

Our point guard didn't waver. "Live in the moment, laddy. All that matters right now is that Ling-Ling likes popcorn. Her name means 'soul' and 'clever.' 'Bell and chime.'"

Our basketball season was in the crapper. Everyone was frustrated. We kept getting creamed by bigger and better schools, and I wasn't making Coach too chipper with my plummeting free-throw percentage. Whenever he became super angry, though, like when our power forward mouthed off at practice about Coach really needing a cigarette, his method of choice was "Mr. Happy," a rhetorical device of seasoned oak into which he'd drilled holes for aerodynamic speed. Our forward got even by scraping off the filling in Coach's file cabinet Oreos stash and replacing it with braunschweiger.

The final straw was when Coach paddled Poindexter for cursing. Vannerson sometimes swore a blue streak himself, so that was like Widow Douglas getting on Huck for smoking his corncob pipe while she huffed snuff. Those licks hurt! Our star player. Suffice to say, there was a rather complete gibbous-moon harvest at Vannerson's winesap apple orchard by all the starters. One day dozens of trees chock-full. Next morning, no apples. Psy-ops, right? Had to defend ourselves. Imagine his face at dawn.

"Ms. Johnson is oblivious, lost on some nineteenth century moor or heath. I'll saunter to the bathroom, fill the sucker with oil and popcorn. We'll wait for the vice principal's hourly hall sweeps, then you go and turn it on."

"Okay," I agreed.

Bobby Russell said a quick prayer.

"God help us!"

So the die was cast. Poindexter's mother was a registered nurse, and he almost ruined matters from the get-go, asking Ms. Johnson if he might possibly have permission to micturate. She glared briefly. But signed. Ten minutes later I hustled down the hallway, flipped the big machine's switch, then boogied back while the popping ensued. What we didn't anticipate was that vice principal Wilkerson and Mrs. Mutchler, who were married to other people, had slipped into her guidance counselor's office for some quick canoodling. They smelled the aroma and sent out a posse.

Once Coach Vannerson had been located, he stormed into the cafeteria screaming: "Poindexter! You and I are going to get to the bottom of this!"

"Pun intended, Coach?"

"Get a move on, buster. I'm going to light you up."

-"Hold it just one second, Bob! This is my study hall!" Ms. Johnson looked livid. "Don't you see these *good* students working?" She indicated Beth and Ling-Ling's trig study session. "Also, this before-the-Flood practice you have of paddling people is bone-headed. Today, I'm putting my foot down."

She wheeled toward my teammates.

"Did you start the popcorn machine, Alan?"

"Yes ma'am."

"Go get me some. While it's fresh and hot."

"Yes ma'am."

"Don't you eat one single kernel, mister. Bob, we can talk more about this in private. Regrets for shouting, but you yelled first. I'll meet you next hour in the teacher's lounge okay?

Following whatever transpired between Ms. Johnson and Coach V. in their teacher's lounge chautauqua, no student ever again got "lit up" by the paddle with holes drilled in it. That Poindexter. ¡Que cojones! Sure, he had to write a research paper on George Eliot or Emily Brontë. Due in two weeks. Ms. Johnson was a taskmaster, but fair and open-minded. He agreed to twelve pages, but only if she would read J. D. Salinger's masterpiece set in a *really* messed-up school. They cut a deal.

But we basketball players still got zilch, popcorn-wise. ◆

The Tao of Weighing In

BETH LEVINE

The Way to Weigh:

1. First thing in the morning. (Better yet, while you're still asleep. Maybe you're dreaming!)
2. *After* you've pooped/peed and *before* you've eaten.
3. Stark naked.
4. *After* you've brushed your teeth (plaque can add pounds) but *before* you've swallowed any water.
5. Lean this way or that to make the scale needle move. Who is to say which is the correct point? And if you need to grab the windowsill to keep your balance? Well, we don't want you should fall.
6. Weight usually varies by a half pound each time you step up. Accept the number that appears two out of three times—unless that's the higher number; in which case, go for three out of five.
7. Subtract a pound if your hair is wet.
8. Subtract two pounds if you are wearing underwear.
9. Subtract four pounds if you've had Chinese food the day before, or actually anytime it's humid outside and your rings are tight.
10. Subtract twenty pounds if you have your period.
11. Never use anyone's scale but your own. Everyone else's is way off, unless it reads thinner. Then *never* use your own again.

If you are being weighed at your doctor's office? A whole other set of rules:
1. Before lunch. If you can only get an appointment after lunch, insist they deduct five pounds.

2. Stripped, or at the very least, without shoes. If forced to wear pants, make sure you take your keys and wallet out of your pockets.

3. After you've given a urine sample.

4. Insist that the nurse wait until the scale arm stops bouncing before she writes it down.

Very important rules about calories that you probably didn't know:

1. If you break food in half, there are no calories.

2. Food you eat from other people's plates has no calories.

3. Food you eat standing up has no calories.

4. If you see a piece of chocolate cake and you don't eat it, you lose weight.

5. If you see a piece of chocolate cake and you don't eat it, you can treat yourself to a piece of chocolate cake later as a reward and you won't gain weight. ◆

Happier Than

ASHLEY CHANTLER

April

The Gate Inn. Mum's reading the dessert menu. I'm necking my fourth pint and considering single malts.

She eventually gets to the final line. "What an odd pudding! Cream, ice cream, or custard."

"No, they go with the three puddings marked with an asterisk. So if you choose the apple crumble, you could have it with cream, ice cream, or custard."

"Right . . ." She begins again, reading from the top, occasionally mouthing the words, and eventually gets to the final line. "Rather strange . . ."

"They go with the first three puddings on the list. If you choose the apple crumble, say, you can have it with cream, ice cream, or custard."

"Right . . . I'm not sure I like chocolate brownie."

There's a long silence.

"I think I might have the . . ."

There's another long silence.

"What does that last line mean?"

"Christ. I've explained that. They're options to go with some of the puddings."

"Right . . ."

"I'm going for a smoke."

I head outside, have a roll-up, return.

"Picked a pudding yet?"

"I'm going to have chocolate brownie."

"Excellent."

"With cream, ice cream, and custard.

July

She's rung again (the third time this week) to check on something.

"When you visited and we were at Reculver, what were those things we saw in the sea?"

"Seals."

"Seals . . ."

"Seals."

"I don't know how to spell that."

"Have you got a pen?"

"Yes."

"Okay. S."

"S . . ."

"E."

"E . . ."

"A."

"A . . ."

"L."

"L . . ."

"S."

"S . . ."

"Seals."

"Seals." Pause. "Are you sure they weren't dolphins?"

September

She turns off the TV, yawns, and stands up. "I'm going to bed. What do you want for your birthday?"

"I've no idea."

"What about a book?"

"OK, I'll have a mull and let you know."

"About what?"

"My birthday present."

"Your birthday's in February!"

"I know."

"You better do."

December

The Fordwich Arms. Our meals have been ordered and I'm trying to think of something to say when Mum takes from her worn "bag for life" a crinkly plastic bottle of water.

"What are you doing?"

"Having some water."

"We're in a pub."

"I know."

"Why don't you drink your lemonade?"

"Because this water," she points at it, "doesn't have bubbles. That lemonade," she points, "is effervescent." She smiles, opens the bottle, and takes a sip.

February

"Hi Mum, it's Ash."

"Why?"

"I was just ringing to thank you for my birthday present."

"Yes . . ."

"It's great. I look forward to reading it."

"I put some scraps out for the fox. I hope he visits."

"I'm sure he will. Some tasty scraps."

"OK, bye."

March

I'll never know what she meant when she said, "I put carrier bags in the bath because the fridge is in the porch." ◆

An Open Letter to a Traveling Salesman, Sugar Camp, Wisconsin, Circa 1996

ANNA VODICKA

To the man who, over the course of a half hour on our doorstep, persuaded my father to purchase a year's supply of classic literature; who may or may not have had any personal interest in classic literature himself; who very well may have been in the door-to-door bookselling business purely for the money, since it was 1996 and there was still sort of money to be had in books; who may have found himself unemployed a year later, when Amazon colonized the universe, but who, that day, may have celebrated with a juicy steak dinner at a nearby supper club, congratulating himself on a home-run pitch to yet another gullible hick; but who, upon collecting Dad's Visa card number and signature, processed the order, money-back-guaranteeing that once a month, two leather-bound volumes arrived on our doorstep in glorious, gilt-edged pairs—*Pride & Prejudice* and *Walden*, *The Scarlet Letter* and *Great Expectations*, *Emma* and *Portrait of the Artist as a Young Man*—packages my dad always saved so that I could open them and order them on the bookshelf, which had previously housed several editions of the Bible and preacher autobiographies like Jim Bakker's *I Was Wrong*; meanwhile, my high school English teacher assigned Agatha Christie and Louis L'Amour in college-bound English and dreamed aloud about being rid of us, tanning, and listening to Jimmy Buffet on some sunny Mexico beach, and spent an entire semester reclined with his feet on the desk, barely sentient while we took turns reading aloud a modernized version of Shakespeare ("Yo, Mercutio! What's up, bro?"), ignoring my impassioned requests to read the original because, he said, we "just weren't smart enough"; and so I returned home at the end of the school day filled with fire, a vindictiveness that would not be in vain, because our home now housed a small library of classic literature, built slowly over the course of that year, and I plucked a volume from the shelf in an act of private teenage rebellion, my reactive state subdued slowly, page by page, through timeless stories; and who, for that reason, will always be my legendary white knight, my literary prince, my mythological hero forever journeying the flat, empty miles of America's Dairyland with a sedan full of catalogs and credit card receipts to avenge the miseducation of angst-ridden youth:

Thank you.
Sincerely,
Anna Vodicka

◆

Résumé of a Desperate College Grad

CANDY SCHULMAN

Objective:

Someone, *anything* to rescue me from my parents' basement!—I'm being held hostage because I'm overeducated, unemployed, and broke.

Highlights of Qualifications:

- Liberal Arts degree, ranked #5 on Forbes's "The 10 Worst College Majors List"

- Four years on a campus overblown with history, intellectual pretension, and tenured professor/underage co-ed affairs

- Conversant in art and literature—when Americans would rather debate Trump versus Cruz

- Multitasker: Can text, Tweet, update Facebook status, Snapchat, post on Instagram, pee, and plagiarize a paper at the same time

- Proficient in college drinking games with knowledge of mixology for Brass Monkeys, instrumental for surviving somniferous corporate meetings

Education:

Hoity-Toity College Too Elite to Divulge, in the middle of nowhere in the Northeast, with less than a 10 percent admissions rate and failed diversity efforts
G.P.A.: Too mediocre to mention (see above, regarding drinking games)
Sports: Trying to elevate Ultimate Frisbee to Varsity status
Leadership Activities: Organized the college's first hot dog eating contest

Community Service: Buying tequila for underage underclassmen who couldn't afford fake IDs

Awards: Campus record for sleeping the most number of hours; 21.25 straight

Work Experience:
Post-College Regression in the Post-Recession: June 2015–Present

Position Title: Non-Emerging Adult Seeking Free Rent

- Grudgingly moved back home with parents after graduation
- Spearheaded family debates facilitating difficult decision of which take-out to order in for dinner
- Partnered with Dad to achieve goal of e-mailing at least five résumés a day
- Initiated a ban on any dinner conversation starting with ". . . and what are you planning to do with the rest of your life?"

Nepotism LLC: Summer 2014

Position Title: Glorified Slave for Daddy's Privately Owned Business

- Completed tedious tasks way beneath my worthless $250,000 diploma without verbal complaints and with minimal procrastinating to check my ex-boyfriend's Facebook status
- Social Media 101, promoting my father's business on that infamous World Wide Web. Welcome to the twenty-first century, Dad!
- Statistical Analysis: Convinced Dad to give me a lift to work 68.5% of the time; limited arguments to 1.5 a day, five days a week.

Camp Privilege / Take a Rich Kid to the Country USA; Summer 2012

Position Title: Assistant Counselor and Glorified Babysitter

- Couldn't score an internship because it was the Great Recession (not my fault, I was *born* into this mess)
- Tirelessly chased whining five-year-olds
- Successfully kept gluten-free and peanut-allergic kids from trading lunches
- Never lost one camper during educational trips, trying not to smile when they taught each other how to curse on the bus.

Previous Black Market Employment: Summer 2011

Position Title: Purebred Dog Walker

- Discovered how people pay more to take care of their pets than their children. (Put *that* on the syllabus for Sociology 200)
- Ironic that an eighteen-year-old can make twenty bucks an hour *cash*, when today's English majors face the prospect of making $12.50 an hour to work in publishing, if it still exists
- This type of fiscal pondering positions me for a job in economics, a field less precise than philosophy, which, did I mention, was my minor? (#4 on the *Forbes* Worst College Major list).
- Skills gained: Picked up hot guys on the street who were impressed that I could walk three English bulldogs without entangling their leashes

Additional Skills & Training:

- Fluent In textbook French, advantageous when avoiding ordering organ meats in a *Rive Gauche* bistro
- Ability to use "ironic" and "disreputable" in a sentence in a vainglorious way

- One-day barista training course. Artery-clogging full fat or tasteless skim in your latte?

- Red Cross Babysitters' Certificate, eighth grade

Other Achievements & Awards:

- Only girl on my dorm floor who didn't gain the Freshman Fifteen

- No history of eating disorders

- Completed marathon: Reread all seven volumes of *Harry Potter*, pausing only for bathroom breaks

- Raised SAT scores 200 points on Adderall

- Won tacky gymnastics medal in third grade—along with everyone else who showed up

- No debt . . . although indebted to my parents for life—which they remind me of every chance they get. As in: "Do you know how many college graduates would rather take out the garbage than pay back their student loans?" ◆

Nipples

FIONA TINWEI LAM

I had noticed them before, of course, on my mother, father, women in changing rooms, men at public swimming pools. I'd glance before turning away in embarrassment. They looked like discolored belly buttons up there on the chest where you weren't supposed to look unless you were rude or a pervert.

But suddenly, when I was around twelve, my nipples started to announce their presence. Before, they'd just seemed like slightly puckered polka dots of tanned skin, or maybe a species of mole. But now they were starting to thicken, becoming—to my horror—more visible, even through my clothes. Puberty was clearly changing everything for the worse.

I was terrified that I'd end up with nipples like my mother's, which were huge dark nubs the color of liver. (My sister and I had been bottle-fed at my mother's insistence during the heyday of infant formula. My mother, the obstetrician, scoffed at my father, the pediatrician, when he dared to offer a different opinion.) One time, when I was eight or nine years old, she proudly squeezed her nipples right in front of me to show me the milk for my baby brother. I already knew that *proper* milk came from cows, was pumped into vats, then cartons, which were shipped to grocery stores, purchased, and put in fridges to be poured for a cool, refreshing beverage to accompany cookies. What came from my mother made me think of pus.

In sixth and seventh grade, I tried to push my nipples down and in, hoping they'd go away. They didn't, so I crossed my arms a lot. In eighth grade I wore layers to hide them, as well as the mortifying outlines of the old, scratchy, ill-fitting bras my mother had dredged up from her ancient stash. First layer, mortifying bra with obtrusive buckles; second layer undershirt; third blouse; fourth T-shirt or cardigan; fifth raincoat, with lining on cold days, or without on warm days. In the first few months of high school, I'd only take off the coat when seated at my desk in the classroom. In phys ed, I would reduce the layers and pray we wouldn't go outside in the cold. By the end of grade eight, I had gradually and cautiously settled on three layers, and even that seemed bordering on wanton. All the other girls were wearing jeans and light cotton tops or sweaters, oblivious to what was revealed—perhaps even proud of their natural endowments. I knew enough not to be proud. Pride was dangerous, as proven by the news clippings about rape that my mother left on the pillow on my bed.

Decades later, when I became a mother myself, my nipples had grown into their genetic inheritance. The mantra now was "the breast is best," as chanted by the midwives, doulas, nurses, parenting magazines, lactation consultants, and La Leche League followers. After I gave birth, so many of these breast experts had scrutinized, grabbed, and manipulated my breasts to instruct me on the proper latching process that my self-consciousness withered away.

All that breastfeeding during the first year left my nipples chafed and stinging. I would keep looking down to see if they were bleeding or about to fall off my chest. For two-and-a-half years I did my duty, praying that my breasts wouldn't become *National Geographic* material. Then much later, I read a *Maclean's* article that stated that breast milk is laden with toxins, especially in the West. One day my kid will accuse me of giving him cancer through misplaced devotion, a fine addition to the list of issues he can discuss with a future therapist. ◆

Bone & Ants

JOSH RUSSELL

My dog got ahold of a chicken bone covered in fire ants. This is a metaphor for pornography. This a metaphor for the time in high school when I read my girlfriend's sister's diary and was sure, though her thirteen-year-old sister's prose was so purple it was hard to translate into a coherent confession, that my girlfriend had had a fling while on a family vacation. This is a metaphor for teenage sexual desire. This is a metaphor for AIDS as depicted in the late-1980s health center pamphlets and posters I saw while an undergraduate at the University of Maryland. This is a metaphor for the will to power. This is a metaphor for the retrospective guilt I felt decades after I stole a few coins from the wicker Sunday school collection plate in the basement of the Baptist church my Marxist parents cleaned every Monday as part of the $75 rent they paid for the foursquare on Mulberry Street in Normal when I was in fourth grade. This is a metaphor for five of the seven deadly sins. This is a metaphor for the time when I was fifteen years old and I was caught shoplifting a paint marker from a drugstore in Wheaton Plaza and it took my dad a long time to come and collect me because he felt it necessary first to shower and put on a tie, and a metaphor for the time my daughter was four years old and stole gum from a drugstore, proudly showed it to Mommy in the parking lot, and had to go back inside and confess her crime. This is a metaphor for Ronald Reagan. This is a metaphor for the Internet. This is a metaphor for free market capitalism. This is a metaphor for populism and fascism. This is a metaphor for consciousness. ◆

The Troubles

BILLY COWAN

I've never forgiven Ma for murdering Bernadette Devlin.

It's 1972 and I'm a six-year-old wee skitter. I've just been given my first goldfish and Ma wants to know what I'm going to call it.

"Bernadette," I say.

"There'll be nae Bernadette in this hoose," my Ma replies.

Being a staunch Ulster-Scots loyalist, my mum hates Bernadette Devlin. She hates all Seans and Patricks and Seamuses and Gerrys as well, but she especially hates Bernadette. I, on the other hand, love her because she's sweet and fierce, at the same time, and she uses big words like proletariat and mandate, and she's not afraid of men in suits because she attacked one in the House of Commons and won't apologize for it.

Ma calls her a sleekit fenian hoor and doesn't want the goldfish to be associated with that, but Da is on my side.

"Fer God's sake, let the wean call his goldfish what he wants!"

And so my first goldfish is christened Bernadette. Ma doesn't say anything more about it, but I can tell she doesn't like it because she never feeds it or plays with it or cleans its bowl.

I've had Bernadette for about three weeks when Ma comes home from the factory with a larger black fish in a plastic bag.

"Ah've got a wee friend for Bernadette," she says.

It has bulbous eyes that make it look stupid. She plops it into the bowl.

"He's called Big Ian."

Ma smiles. She doesn't have to tell me who he's named after. His big grinning face peers down at me from the walls of our living room every day and his big booming voice terrifies me every time I see him on the news, which is all the time.

"They'll be good company for each other," Ma says. And I believe her.

On the third morning after Big Ian's arrival, I come downstairs to feed the fishes before going to school. Bernadette isn't there, but Big Ian is fatter and swimming around slower than usual. My mouth falls open. I dash into the kitchen to tell Ma.

"Never mind, son," says Ma unsurprised. "Why don't Ah get you two more and you can call them Crystal Tipps and Alistair after yer favorite cartoon. Ah'm sure Big Ian won't have anything against them." ◆

Clothes Make the Woman

EUFEMIA FANTETTI

Like Picasso, I also had a blue period, one that was considerably less influential and productive. During that awkward phase—fresh out of my teens—I wore track pants and sweatshirts night and day, seamlessly transitioning from casual sleep attire to ready-to-wear diurnal cozy.

My father, a fashionable Italian immigrant, asked, "Don't you want to look nice?"

My mother, a fashion plate and dedicated practitioner of Retail Therapy, was more direct: "What for the love of God are you wearing?" She begged Jesus to put some sense into me, and petitioned the Holy Virgin for help, wondering what she'd done to deserve such a daughter. "Everyone's going to see you walk down the street and say, 'There goes Lucy's daughter, dressed like a gypsy; poor Lucy.' Can't you see your reflection in the mirror?"

She blamed my careless attitude with apparel on my public school education; they should have sent me to Catholic school, she insisted, even though there was no patron saint for the fashion feeble.

Both my parents were extremely stylish. Strangers admired my mother's matching outfits, her classic purses and shoes. My father's movie star looks were matched by his well-fitted wardrobe. Raised in the Holy Land of Gucci reverence and Versace veneration, they couldn't understand any of my attempts at being chic, a stage that had been delayed several years by my mother's ability to sew. I spent the early part of my childhood wearing handmade dresses; the same bland cut in various fabric patterns, a hideous early-Mormons-inspired dress resembling a Puritan smock that my mother modernized with enormous ruffles. Everyone else was wearing Jordache jeans, running around during recess like they belonged in the era, while I looked like an extra who'd wandered too far from the set of *Little House on the Prairie.*

I rebelled: When I turned sixteen, I went through a pseudo-punk-slash-hippie stage, cutting off all my hair and dying it tar-black with dark blue streaks. The shade of electric blue washed out within a week to a fern-like green that made it look as though I had patches of moss growing around my face. Without knowing about the band, I wore a Dead Kennedys' "Holiday in Cambodia" T-shirt *and* a dyed denim jacket that marked me as a moving target, due to the hastily drawn Mercedes logo on the back that I thought meant peace. I looked like a pale imitation of an anarchist who tripped and fell into a vat of tie-dye.

My parents—and a few innocent bystanders—were horrified. My mother stepped up her efforts to avoid family devastation and ruin, swapping her regular purchases of bedsheets and table linens for my dowry to beaded tops, nightgowns, and negligees: "Men care what you look like, even if you don't." One ensemble she thought particularly fetching was a lacy cerulean teddy and matching kimono-cut robe, a nylon outfit so hazardous to health that it carried a Highly Flammable warning. The packaging advised not to wear the outfit near a stove burner.

"I wouldn't be caught dead in this, unless it's the reason I die," I told her at the unveiling.

"I'm the one who's dying—you're killing me with ugly clothes."

I agreed to go buy myself something nice. With money in my pocket and a mission in mind—to bring back a suitable item, an elegant and versatile piece that would make my parents stop harping—I set off for the mall, the only place to hang out in our suburb. Determined to get my parents off my case, I found a simple black skirt that made me look slim and metropolitan. I hesitated at the counter—the skirt was ankle-length, and flashbacks from my austere-meets-ostentatious period abounded. "What's the return policy?" I asked the cashier.

Back home, I modeled the skirt for my folks.

My mother retreated in silence to make dinner, her shoulders curved in defeat.

My father rubbed his eyes. "Why do you dress like my mother?"

Where I saw urbanite, he saw an elderly Italian peasant. In defiance, I wore it every day for a week.

My mother kept quiet and continued to buy me clothes that went direct to friends or donation bins. My dad would come to accept me as I was; from then on, at my urging, he'd often compliment my great personality. ◆

The Language of Dogs

ADAM FARRER

On our evening walks, my greyhound Betty and I often encounter the same old man and his dog. The man is about five feet tall, while his dog, some kind of mastiff I think, stands almost level with his chest. The dog is male with huge, pendulous balls that swing heavily beneath it like milk-laden udders. Seeing them approach I'm always moved to consider a child walking his cow to market.

But when Betty spots them her reaction is less amused. Her ears scissor in flat against her head and she slows her pace. This is a reaction that I have come to recognise, and empathize with, as in "Oh God. *Him.*"

This happens to everyone from time to time. You lock eyes with a tedious old acquaintance in the street and you feel your heart sink, dreading the awkward conversation that will follow. But while a human has the ability to fake a mobile call and grin apologetically as they pass, a dog has no such option, knowing that even stopping to defecate won't prevent them from being hassled.

This dog's senses don't seem particularly up to par, usually distracted by a patch of another dog's urine or pausing to issue a turd that a horse would be proud of, so it rarely notices us until we're close by. But when it eventually spots us, it more than makes up for its lack of awareness with passion.

"WHORE!" it barks, bassy and emphysemic. Like a hollering drunk. "WHORE!"

The first time this happened I did a mental double take. *Did that dog just call Betty a whore*? Well, he certainly said it. There was no mistaking the word. So clear you could in all good conscience accuse the owner of having taught it. "WHORE! WHORE! WHORE!"

"Come on, now," the owner admonished, heaving on the lead. Grunting through effort as his dog strained to reach us. "Give over. That's enough."

It was like listening to someone trying to calm a troublesome elderly relative. The type who becomes abusive after a few glasses of gin. Who considers themselves to be painfully honest rather than rude.

"Look, I just tell it like it is," this dog might say. "Some people just don't like to hear the truth."

But really, this was no way to treat Betty. Until her retirement she had raced professionally, building up a credible record of wins before being sold for breeding.

When we adopted her we were told "Betty . . . didn't take to breeding," a statement that told a miserable story of her darting fearfully around a pen, desperately shifting her rump away from the hopeful, bucking hips of eager males. Eventually her new owners cut their losses and tossed Betty back over her trainer's wall, leaving her for dead. Or for whatever people think happens to a dog when you dump it over a wall.

So anyone with any decency would think twice about shouting slurs at someone who has suffered such a life. But this dog had no moral concerns.

"WHORE!" it continued, its shouts becoming strangulated as the man leaned back and shortened its lead further. "WHO…"

The word was cut off by a mighty heave that forced the dog to rear up on its hind legs like a dancing bear. But a bear whose greater specialism is cursing. Though in fairness the dog makes a pretty good job of dancing, hopping between its back paws like a chicken on a hot plate. An actor who can dance rather than a dancer who can act.

"I'm sorry," the owner said as we crossed paths.

I leaned in to Betty, rubbing her behind the ear. "He just wants to make friends," I said, compelled to comfort her.

"WHORE!" the dog shouted over its shoulder one final time as it moved into the distance.

I was reminded of the kind of men who try to woo female pedestrians by shouting sexually aggressive slogans from the windows of passing vans.

"I've got a chew toy for ya!"

"Show us all ten of your nipples!"

That sort of thing.

So as we continued on our way, I didn't consider a new walking route or taking Betty out at a different time. Instead I headed home, picked a gravy bone out of her treat jar, and stood over her, holding it high and tantalizing in my hand.

"OK," I said, my voice firm and educational. "Repeat after me. Bite me. Bite me. Bite me . . ." ◆

Tutus Are My Only Friend

SARAH BROUSSARD WEAVER

My second grader's butt is always showing. Always. Don't judge, I'm doing the best I can. This doesn't happen to any of my other kids. I have three other kids but only this one has a rare butt. I can't figure out what is wrong but all jeans, leggings, shorts, and pants that are made for little girls do not fit her right. Sometimes it's just a little crack, sometimes the half moon, but no matter the degree, *she cannot feel that her bottom is hanging out.*

I feel like she should detect the cool breeze on a body part that should not be feeling any cool breezes, but she does not. So I am always like, "Your butt is showing again," and she's always like, "Ugh Mom, stop," and reaches back and gives a small tug that does nothing.

She doesn't care. At all. She only gets aggravated that I am bugging her about it. Anyone would get frustrated at hearing the same thing over and over. Or having to *say* the same thing over and over. But that's called parenting. I can't just ignore my child's bottom showing for all to see—can I? Should I try? It's a nice distracting thought, anyway.

I feel like an awful mother. No good mom would allow her child's bottom to hang out. I have tried her correct size in pants, a size smaller, a size bigger, and two sizes bigger. No pants on this earth—whether made in an inhumane sweatshop or fair-trade, handwoven and stitched by Tibetan monks who fleeced the little free-range organic hand-fed cosleeping sheepies themselves (and I have no doubt there is a tiny shop (made of weathered repurposed Amish barn wood) selling pants like this in Portland, if only I were cool enough to go to the cool shops)—will contain it; her butt *will* be free.

She refuses to wear a belt. I can't blame her for that because even I know that belts were invented by Satan to make people look fatter and feel more uncomfortable and like life is not worth living. The only thing that has worked is making her wear a tutu or skirt over the pants. So yes, that is my kid wearing a totally non-matching fluffy blue tutu over her pink polka-dot pants, even though it's rainy and muddy and we are hiking on a trail (hiking is a requirement in Portland; they'll send you back to California if you don't hike happily). It's better to see a muddy tutu than a muddy butt.

I am sure her bottom is always showing at school, but at least I am not there to see it. And if I don't see it, and the principal doesn't call me, did it really happen? I argue that it did not. But summer is coming, a bottom will be showing, and I will have no refuge. I'm making an online order today for my daughter's new summer shorts. And I better add more tutus. ◆

Permanent Record

JEFF FRIEDMAN

For Dale Abrams

"One more mark on your permanent records, and you'll never get a job," Principal Hugo said, sitting on the throne in his office, reading from the long scrolls of our misdeeds.

While Miss Denny shook her head skeptically, Dale Abrams and I vowed to do better. But later that day, when Sonny Linder did another one of his famous somersaults down the steps, we shouted, "Man down, man down."

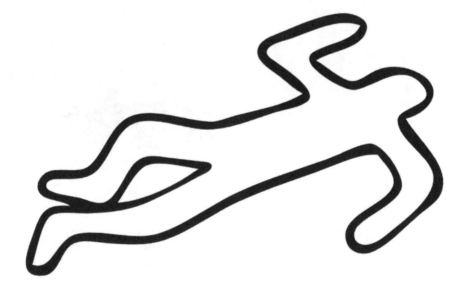

Miss Denny left her post at the doorway, pronto. As she kneeled over the body, we peered over her shoulder. Dale held up his hand like a referee and began counting, "1, 2, 3 . . . 10, and the winner by a knockout—Miss Denny!"

She swore at us in Latin, then issued a command: "Get help."

"I think she means you, Dale," I said.

"But she's looking at you," he answered. Since we couldn't figure out which of us she was talking to, we decided it was best to stay where we were.

Miss Denny laid her head on Linder's chest, listening for a heartbeat. "He's in a coma," she stated as though she were Dr. Kildare.

"What's a coma?" Dale asked.

"That's a tough one," I replied. "I missed it on my SATs."

Miss Denny gave us an evil look. "Get help now or you'll spend the rest of your lives in Detention."

Linder's head rolled to the side, and his tongue flopped out. Bubbles of foam floated from his mouth, but we didn't budge.

Exasperated, Miss Denny huffed, "Watch him or else," and ran down the hallway on her tipsy heels.

"Let's keep an eye on him," I said. We walked over to where Linder lay and nudged him with our feet. Dale put two fingers on the side of his neck.

"He's got a pulse. He must not be dead."

Linder's eyes popped open. Then he jumped up and ran out the door. Now the body was missing, so we had no choice but to chase after him, our permanent records waiting for yet another mark against us. ◆

If I Wrote About My Day Like a Baseball Writer

MARY COLLINS

If I Wrote About My Day Like a Baseball Writer

After a stirring opening morning breakfast of cereal with blueberries and pecans, I gave up my hot morning Irish tea with milk for a forty-five-minute bike ride, which I closed out at 7:55 a.m., before walking through the parking lot at the MDC Reservoir #6 to meet Elizabeth Brewer, formerly with Cleveland, for a one-hour walk with a lot of change-up in the pace, on the inside of the three-mile loop.

If I Wrote About My Day Like Chance the Rapper

I gotta move my old knees slowly
Take the pedals on my feet like they're holy
I've been waiting on this all week
To bicycle through a summer morn to meet
My friend, who's another word-hugging teach.

If I Wrote About My Day Like the New York Times

Mary Collins of West Hartford, CT, met CCSU Professor Elizabeth Brewer for a walk at Reservoir #6 on Farmington Avenue to discuss establishing a new statewide writing contest for high school students.

"There used to be a really exciting program but they lost their funding, so now there's a vacuum that I feel we can fill and also raise the profile of CCSU's writing program."

Brewer concurred.

If I Wrote About My Day Like My High School English Teacher

After eating a breakfast of cereal with pecans and blueberries, (subject of the next phrase must be "I" or you will have a dangling modifier here), I rushed off without my regular cup of Irish Breakfast tea to bike to the reservoir to meet a close friend for a walk (a bit of a run-on; consider breaking this line into two sentences). ◆

Self-Portrait: Questionnaire

MARCIA ALDRICH

1. **What category do your bad dreams fall into?**
   a. Car troubles
   b. Faulty machinery in general, including computers
   c. Being chased
   d. Falling
   e. Trapped

2. **If you chose trapped, where were you trapped?**
   a. In a closet in the library of your elementary school
   b. In a corn combine on your neighbor's farm
   c. Under the weight of the neighbor boy
   d. Under the ice on the river
   e. Behind the yellow school bus doors that wouldn't open

3. **What do you dislike about your current job?**
   a. The pay
   b. The hours
   c. The people
   d. The workplace
   e. The work
   f. All of the above

4. **How do you cope?**
   a. Yelling at strangers in the car
   b. Going ten miles slower than the speed limit
   c. Putting chewing gum on walls and under seats
   d. Reading about extinct species
   e. Dancing when the local football team loses

5. What is your least favorite activity?

   a. Yard work
   b. Meetings
   c. Paying bills
   d. Cleaning the gutters
   e. Overseeing children's homework
   f. Filling out annual reports

6. What word describes your view of mankind at this point in your life?

   a. Joyful
   b. Enlightened
   c. Robotic
   d. Bankrupt
   e. Whiny
   f. Trapped

7. What issue most concerns you?

   a. The state of the economy and your children's future
   b. The state of the economy (I have no children)
   c. Yard waste
   d. Won-lost record of the local football franchise
   e. The disappearance of bees
   f. Being trapped

8. If you had it to do over again, what describes your attitude about having children?

   a. I'd have more
   b. I'd have exactly what I have
   c. I wouldn't have any
   d. I'd have some for others
   e. I'd adopt
   f. I'd get an aquarium

9. **If you have a partner, what noun describes your current feelings?**

   a. Admiration
   b. Resignation
   c. Indifference
   d. Hostility
   e. Suspicion
   f. All of the above plus trapped

10. **At what point did your feelings for your partner change, if they did?**

   a. Shortly after the start
   b. After the first child
   c. After the second child
   d. Recently
   e. Before you began
   f. All of the above

11. **For a holiday gift, which would you prefer to receive?**

   a. Scrooge Mini-Nutcracker
   b. Bavarian Santa Nutcracker
   c. The Bob Cratchit Nutcracker
   d. Animated Musical Toy Chest playing "Rudolph the Red-Nosed Reindeer"
   e. Chinese rickshaw

12. **Which of the following wouldn't you like to receive?**

   a. The Horticultural Institute's Tiered Floral Display
   b. Handmade Kathe Kruse Margretchen Doll
   c. The Lorenzi Cigar Rest with Continuous Burning Wick
   d. Policeman's bullhorn

13. **Which of the following objects suggests your essence?**

   a. Cordless insect vacuum
   b. Body fat analyzer
   c. Step-on garbage pail

    d. Long-reach bulb changer

    e. Stop-Mud-in-Its-Tracks slippers

    f. Washable leather potholders

14. How would you describe your experience taking this questionnaire?

    a. Excited, like watching a Shirley Temple movie

    b. Comfortable, like easing into your La-Z-Boy chair

    c. Expectant, like seeing the mail truck pull in

    d. Bored, like taking notes at a meeting

    e. Sad, like reading the obituary of someone you once loved

    f. Trapped, like required counseling ◆

The Mysterious Case of the Deluded Reader

DAMHNAIT MONAGHAN

Assignment: Write an essay on crime fiction.

Why does the reader care about a fictional crime?

This reader doesn't. It's not my genre. I don't read crime fiction.

Is that your statement?

My statement? Uhm, no. It's the opening sentence for this damn essay I have to write.

Call it what you may, but I'd like to ask you a few questions about it. We're looking into the popularity of crime fiction and you may be of some assistance to our investigation.

I really don't see how I can help. As I said, it's not my genre.

Mmm hmmm. We'd still like to ask you a few questions, just to assist the investigation. You do want to help us, don't you?

Well, yes, but, as I said—

Just a few questions. It won't take long. Sit down, please. You won't mind if I record our conversation. Now, what sort of books did you read as a child?

I read widely across many genres.

Including mysteries.

Ye . . . es.

Isn't it true that you read every single Nancy Drew mystery, in strict numerical order?

Well, yes, but, I was just a kid. I didn't know any better.

And once you had finished with Nancy, you didn't stop there. Your little reading spree continued. You pilfered your brother's Hardy Boy mysteries, didn't you?

. . .

I'll take your silence as agreement. And isn't it also true that by the time you were twelve your appetite for murder had grown?

What the hell do you mean by that?

Well, by then you were devouring Agatha Christie mysteries? Not to mention Sherlock Holmes?

Look, I'm not sure what you're trying to imply, but—

I'm going to read you something I found on your computer hard drive.

What?! You had no right to—

I think you'll find we had every right. Now shut up and listen.

"Although I preferred modest Miss Marple to the preening Poirot, I read them all. And it is truly amazing how some of the images from those book covers stayed with me: I can still see Nancy Drew creeping down a narrow flight of stairs, flashlight in hand, on the cover of The Hidden Staircase; I can vividly recall the dead blonde, sprawled across the floor in a floozy's dress, in Agatha Christie's The Body in the Library."

Your words?

[wipes sweat from brow] Yes, but I was trying to write what the tutor wanted, I didn't really mean it.

So you write a piece on your computer about the staying power of those books but now you claim that you don't read crime fiction. Were you lying then, or are you lying now?

I'm not going to answer that!

Now, more recently, you've read some PD James, a few Ian Rankin, and the occasional Sue Grafton. Am I right?

Well, yeah, but I didn't consciously . . . I mean, they were at the beach house. I, I just picked them up and before I knew it—

You. Just. Picked. Them. Up. That's right. And before you knew it, you'd taken them in your bare hands, wrung every last word out of them, and then tossed them aside. Isn't that right?

Yes. I mean, No! I mean . . . Can I call my lawyer? ◆

Mortifying Metamorphosis

LETA SELETZKY

As a young girl, I abhorred the idea of childbirth. It seemed so violent, so catastrophic. I hoped that by the time I was a grownup, scientists would've invented robots that incubated and bore babies. It would be the 1990s, and anything would be possible.

At the same time, I was ambivalent about the process of physically growing into womanhood. On one hand, I was embarrassed when my mom noted the changes in my body: the rounding, the hair. On the other hand, I eagerly awaited breasts. Would that womanhood entailed only breasts, high heels, and maybe a white Corvette—a sublime existence like that of my mom's friend, Gwen. (I was in awe of her; she was like one of my Barbies come to life.)

The reality was far less glamorous. When my mom curtly informed me one warm afternoon that I now needed to wear deodorant, I was chagrined. And I needed a training bra. What an insult. Exactly how much training would wearing a real bra entail?

Plus, my body seemed to be changing all willy-nilly, not in the graceful and orderly fashion that I would have chosen. Before I had any semblance of the curves I anticipated, I was beset by the less charming markers of maturity, e.g., acne and the aforementioned hair. Then I finally completed training for a real bra. For the first time, my mom took me shopping in the juniors' department—I'd outgrown the children's sizes. Delighted by this upgrade, I tried on a knee-length stonewashed denim skirt. The waist fit fine, but the excess fabric in the hip area flared around me like jodhpurs.

I got my first period at the age of twelve while I was watching *The Muppet Show* with my little brother. In the bathroom, as I frantically tried to figure out what to do, I knew that nothing would ever be the same. Minutes earlier, I was a carefree kid like my little brother. I'd crossed a gulf.

Many years later, after the scientific community's failure to develop and market childbearing robots in the 1990s, I bore a child myself. I had another one two years later. As it turned out, all of those peculiar, thrilling, worrisome bodily changes that I experienced so long ago had a practical application. I'm glad those robots that I hoped for as a young girl weren't available. ◆

We Shall Find Out

ANDREW HUDGINS

One of the few reasons I ventured into my father's bathroom is that he kept the washer and dryer there. The room was as clean as an eighty-eight-year-old man with failing vision could make it, but that's not the same thing as *clean*. Once, while waiting for the spin cycle to finish, I flipped open Dad's electric razor. Each of the three rotary blades was encircled by a solid block of hair—white hair so solidly packed that cleaning the razor took twenty minutes, a constant stream of hot water, my fingernails, and the tines of a fork I smuggled out of the kitchen. My gag reflex also got a thorough workout, but you don't insult a retired air force officer by letting him know you are cleaning up after him.

The only other time I entered my father's bathroom was every single time I entered his house. My brother had long ago observed that when you walked into Dad's house, you called out, "Hey, Pop," walked down the hall to his bathroom, flushed the toilet, and turned on the vent fan before returning to the living room where he was listening to contemporary Christian music at ear-damaging volume. I'd assumed he didn't flush the toilet because, a child of the Great Depression, he was saving money. After all, my mother, another child of that same depression and also a student of water and power bills, used to fuss at my three brothers and me, "You boys don't need to flush the durn toilet every single time you shake the dew off your lilies." She was of the if-it's-yellow-let-it-mellow school of financial conservation decades before the eco-slogan was rhymed into existence.

The situation at Dad's house, by which I mean the smell, got worse when the bathroom vent fan died. For him, no problem. Like his sight and his hearing, his sense of smell was fading too. He saw no need for a fan, and he was not pleased when for Christmas his sons hired an electrician to install one. He assumed his gift was more for us than him. It was that, yes, but it was also intended as a gift for anyone else who visited him.

"Dad, where's your plunger?" I asked one morning after I had woken to the pervasive smell and attempted to remedy it.

"Oh, no! You didn't flush the toilet did you?"

"Yeah, I flushed the toilet and it's clogged. Where's the plunger?"

"Oh, you shouldn't have done that."

In a far back corner of the garage, serving as a maypole for spiders, was the same wooden-handled plunger we had when I was a boy. Over fifty-five years, the red rubber had set as solid as concrete. I drove to the hardware store, bought a new plunger, and went to work on the clog.

Dad was a man of extremes. Mild extremes, but extremes. When his doctor told him he should eat bananas because his potassium count was low, Dad ate so many he brought on nausea and vomiting from a potassium overload. Hyperkalemia, it's called. When the doctor told him he needed more fiber in his diet, his before-bed drink became a water glass of half orange juice and half Metamucil. The concoction was so thick he drank the first third of it and ate the rest with a spoon, choking as he ate. The doctor said "more fiber," and by golly he was following orders.

His nightcap was the reason I was in his bathroom, leaning over the toilet and pumping on the new plunger.

"You wouldn't have to do all this if you did what I do," he said. "They're too big to flush. I just wait till the afternoon when they get soft and break them up with the toilet brush before flushing."

In "The Old Fools," Philip Larkin asks, "What do they think has happened, the old fools, / To make them like this?" He answers, hauntingly and correctly, "We shall find out."

I've got a new toilet brush and I've inherited the perfectly serviceable plunger I bought for Dad. I'm ready for you, Old Age. Bring it on. ◆

Before We Break for Lunch, Let Me Repeat Everything Already Said at This Meeting At Least Twice

MARK ROOKE

Thanks again, team, for taking time out of a busy Friday to get together for the quarterly review. I can't speak for everyone, but I'm starving! Having you all watch me drone through an endless parade of sales slides sure does work up an appetite. Before we dig into this prematurely set-out buffet, I'd like to take a moment to repeat everything already mentioned in this presentation.

Did I mention our new priority to shift from emerging markets to focus more on adaptive capacity? I did? Twice? Excellent. I'll repeat it again, only this time with uninterpretable MBA jargon like "strategic brand synergy" and "structural technology convergence." By now all interest in what that even means is long gone, along with half of the ice on the beverage cart. On the subject of

beverages, let's heave out some forced laughter for the diet soda joke I'm about to throw at Diane. Fun fact about Diane, everyone: she has diabetes.

Let's revisit these earnings graphs for a third time, partially due to how proud I am of the numbers, but also because the potato salad hasn't sat unrefrigerated long enough. It's not every day our net profits peak the two million mark! And botulism spores need at least an hour at room temperature before they'll colonize the mayonnaise. Could you reverse the presentation forty slides, but do it one at a time? Great. At this point, looking at these pie charts for a fourth time is the mental equivalent of drinking our urine, but I'd like to give the office sycophants a chance to grab for relevance.

Speak of the devil! Dennis, you have an irrelevant question? I'd be happy to answer it in the most roundabout way possible. I'll start by asking you to repeat it, misinterpreting your wording, then belaboring the point until the buns on those barbecue sliders become soggy enough to lose their integrity.

And speaking of lost integrity, all revenue gained from these recent sales will suspiciously disappear after management takes more than its share, not unlike the chocolate chip cookies next to the chip basket. The income generated here will in no way improve office conditions or performance expectations. Your limited budgets will remain stagnant—as stagnant as that Brunswick stew that's visibly striated after not being stirred for two hours.

Whoa there, Mike! Do I need to bring baggies of Cheerios to the next quarterly review? Unless you brought enough granola bars for everyone, let's hold off a minute. Here's a comment about how snacking during meetings is unprofessional, darkly peppered with hints that premature attempts at my potty training warped me into a pushy adult who associates others' obedience with self-worth. Or maybe I just hate my dad. Who knows? Bottom line is nothing pleases me more than pressuring a room of grown adults to suffer solely because I can. So, let's put that Clif Bar away for now, alright Mike? Thanks.

Alright then, who else is ready to eat? Good. But before we break for lunch, let me repeat everything already said at this meeting at least twice. ◆

Prompts and Suggestions

We asked a few of our *Flash Funny* authors to reflect (in flash form) on the process of writing both funny and brief. The answers appear below, followed by a few prompts and ideas for writing your own flash nonfiction funnies.

Get In, Leave Holes, Punch, Get Out

BY LISA ROMEO

When I write flash (serious or, hopefully, humorous), I work differently from the way I build longer pieces. I work slowly, one word, phrase, sentence at a time, not moving on until I think those words, phrases, sentences capture what I intend, packed with information, power, emotion—or a punchline.

It's not that when I'm writing something longer I allow flabby, empty passages through to the finished work (at least I hope not). But with flash I'm stricter, insistent those I'll-revise-it-later sentences don't appear even in crappy first drafts. Humor is all about timing, and on the page, humor writing depends on well-timed, mercilessly pruned word pictures.

To write something short but good takes me a long time (Blaise Pascal and Mark Twain be praised). I move slowly through fewer words, polishing to what I hope is shiny succinctness. I'm looking for what I can omit—not because it's not important, but because it is. Flash often asks readers to see something by way of what's not there. It's my job to place holes strategically so the *aha* (or holy hell!) moments belong to readers, pulling them deeper into the piece that will soon spit them right back out.

I choose flash when I want to get in and get out, when I've decided a story, topic, or experience is best told without dwelling. I want to lure a reader in with a swift but fleeting punch to the gut—and hope the punch lingers. And, sometimes, hurts.

Timing, Timing, Timing
BY SVEN BIRKERTS

A flash question gets a flash (probably not flashy) response. But it's an interesting question. I'd never thought whether my writing "process"—if we can ennoble it thus—is the same for longer and shorter pieces. Once I gave it a moment's thought, however, I realized that it is. Essays over, say, a thousand words most certainly need a scaffold—not only a linguistic inspiration of some sort, but a structural one as well (the two often appear mysteriously in tandem). Whereas short flash essays, or whatever we want to call them, can, and usually do, arrive on a whim and ride their way to conclusion via the local inspirations of language, metaphorically related to what Frost wrote: "Like a piece of ice on a hot stove the poem must ride on its own melting." The melting, for me, is the action of rhythm and word sound. Short pieces are governed by the immediacy of their local interactions. Their payoffs are not capital-T Thematic, but lowercase: insight and pleasure caught on the wing. One can almost get away without a governing structure, though maybe not quite. Oops, my time is up. Yes, this followed the logic of "flash."

How I Wrote "What Fathers Say, What Daughters Hear"
BY CHARLES RAFFERTY

My essay came easily, which is unusual for me. I'm typically a diligent reviser, and I don't mind if a piece takes months or even years to complete.

I'm a father of two daughters, so I had an abundance of material to draw on. Once I struck upon the idea of how easily and how often we miscommunicate, it was a simple matter of generating as many instances as possible. Over the course of a few days, I was able to write about a dozen pages of these "I said/they hear" constructions.

Why didn't I keep going? I had begun to bore myself. Sometimes that's an indication that you're on the threshold of a great discovery. Dead ends can push us to take the work in a completely new direction—potentially hitting upon an even denser vein of silver. That proved not to be the case here, and I put the essay aside for a couple of weeks.

This leaving-it-alone phase is an important part of everything I write. Putting a little distance between myself and the first draft enables me to look at the material with fresh eyes—which, in this case, meant being able to see where I wasn't as funny as I thought I was, or where I had come off sounding more juvenile than I intended.

I'm someone who finds revising much easier than writing first drafts. I've become ruthless in my old age, and I derive great satisfaction from deleting in their entirety the paragraphs I labored over. So it was easy to take a first draft that was twelve pages long and distill it down to four.

Once I'd done that, it was a matter of organizing the moments. I decided that a roughly chronological arrangement would serve the material best.

A Little Bit Funny: On Writing the Flash-Humor Essay

BY LISE FUNDERBURG

I blame my 138-word essay, "What Bad Owners Say at the Dog Park," on photographer James Casebere. We met some years back at an artists' colony, where he crafted funnel clouds out of wire, a far cry from the meticulously constructed dioramas he shoots. "I'm expanding my practice," he explained. The phrase has stuck with me since—it's permission to explore rather than perfect.

My writerly comfort zone is narrative nonfiction, 1,000 to 100,000 words. Recently, I decided to explore ala James while I was in a holding pattern, waiting to hear back from editors and publishers on larger projects. Part of the origin story for the essay is that I was a writer in search of material when I happened to hear some of those irksome dog-park comments for the gazillionth time. Being both annoyed and amused is like muse juice to me, and before you could say "poop bag," I was compiling a list of quotes.

I chose the list format because it would keep me from overwriting: The quotes didn't need a setup beyond the title and, let's be honest, my topic was narrow in scope. Shorter was sharper; sharper was stronger. Lists can provide broad sweeps of information about character, place, or relationships, but as I tell students, lists demand a kind of internal integrity that should be respected and carefully built. I don't believe in random ordering. I'll haphazardly gather my thoughts in a first draft, but then I go back and rearrange for a better arc or tension or rhythm. In this case, I wanted a sense of descending into chaos and self-delusion that would mirror the actual experience.

About "Playing the Chicken"
BY MEG POKRASS

I was born in Pennsylvania but moved to Southern California when I was five. In perfect Santa Barbara, I always felt like a fish out of water. Being in theater helped me overcome my social anxiety, and I became a serious acting student in a land of perfect-looking blonds. They got the best roles because they were confident and appealing. I studied and worked hard memorizing and analyzing character intention, but it never paid off. At the same time, my much older sister was a TV actress, becoming famous, and my middle-school acting teacher had a fan-crush on her. He always said to tell her "hi" for him, and to invite her into class! He seemed to take her non-interest in him out on me personally by casting me in roles nobody would want.

My process is to write quickly and unselfconsciously to produce a first draft. When I wrote this piece, I did not intend to make it funny. It was when I reread my first draft that I realized it had humorous potential, and so I consciously worked in the editing process to bring that out.

Being cast as a chicken (or a dog, or a broom, or a dead body) time and time again by a vain middle-school acting teacher became (with distance) something comical. Readers identify with the idea of not being appreciated or taken seriously and it's gratifying to laugh about the absurdity inherent in such a predicament.

How to Write Comedy
BY ALLISON K. WILLIAMS

1. Practice creativity. Take an improv workshop and learn to say yes to your own ideas. Riff on a bad movie with friends. Play verbal improv games solo in the car, using billboards for "audience suggestions."

2. Practice concision. Write sharp, tight social media statuses. If you have a mildly funny conversation, replay it in your head—anything you can rephrase or edit to be funnier?

3. Actively notice comedy in the world. Mean girls wearing WWJD bracelets. Walla Walla, Washington. Notice how clashing expectations drive humor, especially in sitcoms. Someone under a false impression humiliates themselves—in a way that would be totally reasonable if their understanding was correct. *The Big Bang Theory*'s Sheldon thinks he's the center of the universe and everyone else misunderstands him. To himself, he's a tragic hero. For the audience, he's hilariously oblivious. There's an old vaudeville saying: Tragedy is when I slip on a banana peel. Comedy is when you fall down a manhole and die. That is, Comedy is Tragedy happening to other people. Be that other person for your reader.

4. Use strong consonant sounds—pickle, jackpot. End sentences with concrete nouns and verbs, and with sharp sounds—not "you children" but "you kids." Dialogue tags before punchlines—"And then he said, bada-boom!" Rule of threes—fail, fail, succeed in an unexpected way. Rule of forty-sevens—flog a joke to death and cycle through not-funny to funny-again.

5. Analyze. Ask why. What made that story funny? The visual, the delivery, the underlying premise? Try out mean jabs and folksy yarns and edgy scenarios and family-friendly tales. Read your work out loud and see what makes people laugh.

6. Return to step one. Repeat until you're funny. ◆

More Prompts and Ideas

- **Humor is so often about miscommunication.** Rafferty explores the amusing disconnect between what a father says to his young daughters and what he means—No more TV until I leave for work or take a shower. What other relationships can you mine for hilarity? Is it different with sons and mothers? Different with grandparents? Different between romantic partners? What does your car mechanic say to you, and what does he really mean?

- **Funderberg discusses the way lists work in humor.** Try constructing your own, perhaps finding variations on her title: What _____s Say at the _____. Remember to write more than you need, and then cut the boring parts.

- **Pokrass chronicles the embarrassment of feeling** "lumpy, short, and invisible" on stage and in acting classes. What memories of your younger life contain the same sort of embarrassment? Remember that people are more likely to laugh along when you are poking gentle fun at yourself, not just at others.

- **Both Romeo and Birkerts remind us that humor** (and flash) are all about timing. Effective versus ineffective timing is often detected better by the ear than the logical brain, so make it a habit to read your humorous work out loud, to yourself, and to others, while revising. If a joke is falling flat, often your ear will tell you so.

- **Why is Walla Walla, Washington, funny to say, or hear**? How about pickle? Have you ever found yourself in a pickle in Walla Walla? Words can be funny in and of themselves, and they can make excellent starting points. What words sound funny to you? Labradoodle? Write them down when they occur to you, and let them be your prompt.

- **What is the stupidest thing** you've heard yourself say this week?

- **Tell us about your worst date**—not the disappointing person you were on the date with, but the awkward, cringe-worthy thing you did. ◆

Contributors

Kim Addonizio is the author of a dozen books, most recently *Bukowski in a Sundress: Confessions from a Writing Life* (Penguin), and a poetry collection, *Mortal Trash* (W. W. Norton). Her essays have appeared in the *New York Times*, *The Sun*, *New Letters*, *Narrative*, and elsewhere. She is an occasional presenter for BBC Radio. She lives in Oakland, California, and is online at www.kimaddonizio.com.

Marcia Aldrich is the author of the free memoir *Girl Rearing*, published by W. W. Norton. She has been the editor of *Fourth Genre: Explorations in Nonfiction*. *Companion to an Untold Story* won the AWP Award in Creative Nonfiction. She is the editor of *Waveform: Twenty-First-Century Essays by Women*, published by the University of Georgia Press. Her email is aldrich@msu.edu.

Gina Barreca was hailed as "smart and funny" by *People* magazine, and deemed a "feminist humor maven" by *Ms. Magazine*. Professor of English at the University of Connecticut, Barreca is the author most recently of *If You Lean In, Will Men Just Look Down Your Blouse?* She is also author of *It's Not That I'm Bitter, Or How I Learned to Stop Worrying About Visible Panty Lines and Conquered the World*, the bestselling *They Used to Call Me Snow White . . . But I Drifted: Women's Strategic Use of Humor*, and *Babes in Boyland: A Personal History of Coeducation in the Ivy League*.

Paul Beckman has four story collections, a novella, and a new collection, *Kiss Kiss*. He's had over 350 of his stories published in print, online, and via audio. Paul runs the monthly FBomb NY flash fiction reading series at KGB. He had a story selected for the 2018 Norton *New Micro: Exceptionally Short Fiction* anthology.

Brian Bedard is emeritus professor of English at the University of South Dakota, where he taught from 1990 to 2011. His short stories have appeared in *Quarterly West, North American Review, Alaska Quarterly Review*, and many other journals. His second collection of stories, *Grieving on the Run*, won the Serena McDonald Kennedy Award for Short Fiction from Snake Nation Press in 2008. His short nonfiction piece in this collection is based on his experiences as a produce worker in grocery stores in Utah in the 1970s and '80s. Brian lives with his wife, Sharon, in Spokane, Washington, where he is a member of the English Department at Gonzaga University.

Chelsea Biondolillo is the author of two flash nonfiction chapbooks, *Ologies* and *#Lovesong*. Her work has appeared in a variety of online and print publications and has been collected in *The Best American Science and Nature Writing 2016, Waveform: Twenty-first Century Essays by Women*, and others. She was eventually accepted into graduate school, and now teaches writing at night to support her own essaying habit. She lives outside of Portland, Oregon, with two imaginary cats and an imaginary dog.

Sven Birkerts is the author of ten books of essays and memoir, most recently *Changing the Subject: Art and Attention in the Internet Age* and *The Other Walk*. Formerly director of the Bennington Writing Seminars, he edits the journal *AGNI*.

Douglass Bourne has written many award-winning screenplays, and his essays and poetry have been published in magazine and anthologies. He serves as the screenwriting contest coordinator for a film festival and teaches writing classes at a university.

Caitlin Brady is a writer from south Texas who received her MFA from Columbia University. Her short humor has been published online in *The Columbia Journal, McSweeney's Internet Tendency*, and *The Hairpin*. She lives in New York.

Wendy Brenner is the author of two books of fiction. Her essays and stories have appeared in *The Best American Essays, Best American Magazine Writing, New Stories from the South*, and many magazines. She is a recipient of the National Endowment for the Arts Fellowship, North Carolina Arts Council Fellowship, and the Flannery O'Connor Award for Short Fiction. She teaches at University of North Carolina Wilmington.

Mark Budman was born in the former Soviet Union. His writing has appeared in *Five Points, PEN, American Scholar, Huffington Post, World Literature Today, Daily Science Fiction, Mississippi Review, Virginia Quarterly, The London Magazine* (UK), *McSweeney's, Sonora Review, Another Chicago, Sou'wester, Southeast Review, Mid-American Review, Painted Bride Quarterly, Short Fiction* (UK), and elsewhere. He is the publisher of the flash fiction magazine *Vestal Review*. His novel *My Life at First Try* was published by Counterpoint Press. He has coedited flash fiction anthologies from Ooligan Press and Persea Books. http://markbudman.com

Dani Burlison is the author of *Dendrophilia and Other Social Taboos: True Stories*, a collection of essays that first appeared in her *McSweeney's Internet Tendency* column of the same name, and the *Lady Parts* series (Pioneers Press). She has been a staff writer at a Bay Area alt-weekly, a book reviewer for *Los Angeles Review*, and a regular contributor at *Chicago Tribune, KQED Arts, The Rumpus*, and *Made Local Magazine*. Her writing can also be found at *WIRED, Vice, Utne, Ploughshares, Hip Mama Magazine, Rad Dad, Spirituality & Health Magazine, Shareable, Tahoma Literary Review, Prick of the Spindle*, and more. Dani lives in Santa Rosa, California.

Ron Carlson's selected stories appear in *A Kind of Flying*. His most recent novel is *Return to Oakpine*.

Liane Kupferberg Carter is a nationally known writer, journalist, and advocate for the autism community. Her work has been published in the *New York Times, Washington Post, Chicago Tribune, Brevity*, and many book anthologies. Her memoir, *Ketchup Is My Favorite Vegetable: A Family Grows Up With Autism*, is a winner of a 2017 American Society of Journalists and Authors Outstanding Book award. For more, please visit www.lianekcarter.com.

Ashley Chantler is codirector of the International Flash Fiction Association (IFFA), and coeditor of *Flash: The International Short-Short Story Magazine* and Flash: The International Short-Short Story Press.

Mary Collins spends too much time writing serious nonfiction books on topics like raising a transgender son, or looking at why Americans don't do enough physical activity; she's so grateful for the chance to write something funny (at least she hopes you find it funny). She worked as a writer and editor for twenty-five years in Washington, D.C., for all sorts of clients, but especially for *National Geographic* (on everything from orangutans to the Wright Brothers) and *Smithsonian* (from O'Keefe to the space shuttle). She is a professor of Narrative Nonfiction at Central Connecticut State University.

Josh Couvares was raised in Manchester, Connecticut, and went on to study English and Economics at the University of Connecticut. His work has appeared in the *Long River Review* and the *Hartford Courant*. He currently works and lives in New York City.

Billy Cowan is an award-winning playwright and creative writing lecturer at Edge Hill University, UK. Wanting secretly to be a novelist, but worried about the commitment, he has started to dip his toes into short fiction. Stories have appeared in *Flash: The International Short Short Story Magazine*, and *Quickies 2&3*, published by Arsenal Pulp Press. A new nonfiction piece, "Dig If U Will the Picture," about growing up as a teenage Prince fan, will appear in an anthology entitled *Purple Reign*, published by Salford University.

Renée E. D'Aoust's *Body of a Dancer* (Etruscan Press) was a Foreword Reviews "Book of the Year" finalist. Seven essays have been named "Notable" by *Best American Essays,* and Sundress Publications named "Gratitude is my Terrain," published by *Sweet: A Literary Confection,* one of "2016's 30 Most Transformative Essays." D'Aoust teaches online at Casper College and North Idaho College, and she lives in Switzerland. Please visit www.reneedaoust. com and follow her @idahobuzzy, where she tweets about her mini-dachshund Tootsie.

Helena de Bres writes personal essays, short stories, and humor pieces. She has attended the Bread Loaf, *Tin House*, and *Kenyon Review* writers' conferences, and published work in *McSweeney's Internet Tendency* and *The Rumpus*. Her day job is as an associate professor at Wellesley College, where she teaches ethics, political philosophy, and philosophy of literature.

Brian Doyle was the longtime editor of *Portland Magazine* at the University of Portland, Oregon, and was the author of six collections of essays, two nonfiction books, two collections of "proems," the short story collection *Bin Laden's Bald Spot*, the novella *Cat's Foot*, and the novels *Mink River*, *The Plover*, and *Martin Marten*. Doyle's books have seven times been finalists for the Oregon Book Award, and his essays have appeared in *The Atlantic Monthly*, *Harper's*, *Orion*, *The American Scholar*, *The Sun*, *The Georgia Review*, and in newspapers and magazines around the world. Brian passed away in May 2017, and he is greatly missed.

B. A. East is an author and diplomat. His first novel, *Two Pumps for the Body Man*, did for American diplomacy in the War on Terror what *Catch-22* did for military logic in World War II: The enemy can't kill us if our institutions kill us first. His second novel, *Patchworks*, examines American government and gun culture in a similar light. Ben posts black humor at www.BenEastBooks.com, expressing views that don't necessarily reflect the views of his employer.

Sarah Einstein is the author of *Mot: A Memoir* (University of Georgia Press; 2015) and *Remnants of Passion* (Shebooks; 2014). Her essays and short stories have appeared in *The Sun*, *Ninth Letter*, *PANK* and other journals. Her work has been awarded a Pushcart Prize, a Best of the Net, and the AWP Prize in Creative Nonfiction.

Eufemia Fantetti is a graduate of The Writer's Studio and holds an MFA in Creative Writing from the University of Guelph. Her short fiction collection, *A Recipe for Disaster & Other Unlikely Tales of Love*, was runner-up for the Danuta Gleed Literary Award and winner of the Bressani Prize in 2014. Her writing has been nominated for the Creative Nonfiction Collective Readers' Choice Award and was listed as a notable essay in the 2009 Best American Essay Series. She teaches at Humber College.

Adam Farrer is a writer and spoken word performer based in Manchester, UK. His work has been published by Squawk Back, BBC Online, This Is Not TV, *The Drabble,* and *MacGuffin* and he is the managing editor of creative non-fiction journal and reading series *The Real Story* (therealstory.org).

Terri Favro is a Toronto-based novelist, essayist, and comic book collaborator. Her books include an alternative reality novel, *Sputnik's Children* (ECW; 2017), a spaghetti western-inspired novel, *Once Upon a Time in West Toronto* (Inanna; 2017), and an award-winning novella, *The Proxy Bride* (Quattro; 2012). A nonfiction book about robot-human relationships, *Generation Robot: A Century of Science Fiction, Fact and Speculation* is upcoming in 2018 from Skyhorse Publishing. Terri's stories have appeared in many journals and anthologies, including *Geist, Prism*, and *Clockwork Canada: Steampunk Fiction*. Terri is also the cocreator of the "Bella" series of comics (Grey Borders Books). She is currently working on a steampunk/alt history novel about the War of 1812.

Sam Ferrigno studied English and Creative Writing at the University of Connecticut. His articles have appeared in *Hello Mister*, the *Hartford Courant*, the *Huffington Post* and *Thought Catalog*. He currently lives in Houston where he works as a fundraiser and script reader for the Alley Theatre. He was raised in Pawcatuck, Connecticut, by his endlessly kind parents, grandparents, aunts, and uncles.

Kathryn Fitzpatrick is a student at Central Connecticut State University and a staff reader at the *Adroit Journal*. She is the recipient of a Connecticut Young Writers Trust Award in Prose and a Scholastic Gold Key Finalist. Her work has been featured, or is forthcoming, in *Miscellany, Outrageous Fortune,* and *Fjords Review*, among others. She lives, breathes, and will probably die in Thomaston, Connecticut.

Jeff Friedman's seventh book of poems, *Floating Tales,* was published by Plume Editions/MadHat Press in 2017. He has also cotranslated, with Dzvinia Orlowsky, *Memorials: A Selection by Polish Poet Mieczslaw Jastrun*. Friedman's poems, ministories, and translations have appeared in *American Poetry Review, Poetry, New England Review, Poetry International, Plume, Hotel*

Amerika, Flash Fiction Funny, Agni Online, The New Republic, and numerous other literary magazines. He has received numerous awards and prizes, including a National Endowment Literature Translation Fellowship in 2016 (with Dzvinia Orlowsky) and two individual Artist Grants from New Hampshire Arts Council.

Lise Funderburg is the author of *Pig Candy: Taking My Father South, Taking My Father Home,* a contemplation of life, death, race, and barbecue. She also spearheaded the groundbreaking oral history, *Black, White, Other: Biracial Americans Talk About Race and Identity,* recently released in a twentieth-anniversary edition. Lise's essays have appeared in the *New York Times, Chattahoochee Review, Cleaver, National Geographic, TIME,* and *Brevity,* among other publications. She is a lecturer in creative nonfiction at the University of Pennsylvania and Rutgers University, and a frequent workshop leader in venues ranging from the second floor of a Tokyo coffee shop to the yoga studio across the street from her house. Her website is www.lisefunderburg.com.

Juliana Gray is the author of three poetry collections, most recently *Honeymoon Palsy* (Measure Press; 2017). Her creative nonfiction has appeared in *Waccamaw, Cutbank,* and elsewhere, and her humor writing has been featured in *McSweeney's Internet Tendency, The Belladonna, Splitsider,* and other sites. An Alabama native, she lives in western New York and teaches at Alfred University.

V. Hansmann was raised in suburban New Jersey, growing up to be neurotic, alcoholic, homosexual, and old. For thirty years he worked in an office managing other people's money, and when the office closed, decided to try his hand at nonfiction and poetry. In June 2011, V completed a low-residency MFA in creative writing at the Bennington Writing Seminars. His publishing credits consist of an anecdote in the Metropolitan Diary section of the *New York Times,* essays in *The Common* online, *Brevity, BLOOM, Post Road,* and *Best Travel Writing, Vol. 10,* as well as poems in *Structo, Subtropics, The Tishman Review,* and *The New Guard.* Since August 2011, V has hosted a monthly reading series, Bennington Writers, in Greenwich Village.

Tom Hazuka has published three novels, over sixty-five short stories, and a book of nonfiction, *A Method to March Madness: An Insider's Look at the Final Four.* He has edited or coedited six anthologies of short stories: *Flash Fiction; Flash Fiction Funny; Sudden Flash Youth; You Have Time for This; A Celestial Omnibus: Short Fiction on Faith; Short on Sugar, High on Honey* (UK); and *Best American Flash Fiction of the 21st Century* (Shanghai, China). He teaches fiction writing at Central Connecticut State University. Links to his writing and original songs can be found at tomhazuka.com.

Robin Hemley has published twelve books and has won many awards, including a Guggenheim Fellowship and three Pushcart Prizes. Founder of NonfictioNOW, he is currently Director of Writing at Yale-NUS College in Singapore, professor emeritus at the University of Iowa, and distinguished visiting professor at RMIT in Melbourne, Australia. His website is robinhemley.com.

Denis Horgan is a veteran, award-winning journalist and author who has worked at newspapers in Boston, Dublin, Bangkok, Washington and, most recently at the *Hartford Courant.* His books include: *Sharks in the Bathtub* (collected columns); *Flotsam: A Life in Debris* (essays); *The Dawn of Days* (novel); *Ninety-Eight Point Six* (short stories); and *The Bangkok World* (memoir). He lives in West Hartford, Connecticut.

Nick Hoppe's columns appear every Tuesday in the *San Francisco Chronicle* on the back page of the Datebook Section. His father, former *San Francisco Chronicle* and nationally syndicated columnist Arthur Hoppe, wrote for a living. Fortunately, Nick has other means of support. His topics include business columns relating to the common absurdities of owning a business (he owns restaurants and retail stores throughout California), general lifestyle columns, and travel columns. But no matter what he is writing about, rest assured that he is not taking it too seriously.

Andrew Hudgins is Humanities Distinguished Professor in English Emeritus at Ohio State University, and author of *The Joker: A Memoir,* and nine books of poetry.

Dani Johannesen has a Ph.D. in English from the University of South Dakota, where she studied creative writing and American literature. She currently works as assistant professor in the Liberal Arts & Education Department at the University of Minnesota Crookston. She is coeditor of *Iconic Sports Venues: Persuasion in Public Spaces* (Peter Lang; 2017). Her scholarly and creative work has appeared in *The Nautilus: A Maritime Journal of Literature, History, and Culture*; *South Dakota Review*; *Midwestern Gothic*; *Contemporary South Dakota Women: Influence, Action, and Voice*; *605 Magazine*; and elsewhere.

Jenny Klion's writing has appeared in *Vice's Tonic, Prevention, Purple Clover, The Hairpin*, and Scholastic's *Storyworks*, among others. For her performance work, Ms. Klion received fellowships and grants from NJSCA and NEA/ Rockefeller, as well as a Horton Foote Playwriting Scholarship from HB Studio in New York City. Stage credits include NYC's Lincoln Center, City Center, Alice Tully Hall, Dance Theater Workshop, and more, in addition to one season each with Pickle Family Circus in San Francisco, and Big Apple Circus in NYC.

Fiona Tinwei Lam is the Canadian author of two poetry books and a children's book. Her poetry, fiction, and nonfiction have been published in over thirty anthologies. She is a coeditor of and contributor to the nonfiction anthologies, *Double Lives: Writing and Motherhood*, and *Love Me True: Writers on the Ins and Outs, Ups and Downs of Marriage*. Her poetry videos have been screened at festivals internationally.

Sandra Gail Lambert's memoir, *A Certain Loneliness*, and her novel, *The River's Memory*, are often about the body and its relationship to the natural world. Her writing can also be found in a variety of journals and anthologies including the *Southern Review, Brevity, and Best Women's Travel Writing* Volume 11. She is a 2018 NEA Fellow. Sandra lives with her wife in north-central Florida, close to her beloved rivers and marshes, where she eavesdrops on the chatter of otters and sometimes floats eyeball to nictitating eyelid with alligators.

Sarah Wesley Lemire is an award-winning journalist and monthly humor columnist who writes for *Hartford Magazine* and the *Hartford Courant*, with stories circulated to the *LA Times*, *Chicago Tribune*, and *Baltimore Sun*. Hundreds of her stories appear in print, and her work has been recognized by many local and national organizations, including the Society of Professional Journalists. An overzealous football fan, helicopter parent, and travel junkie, Sarah relocated from Minneapolis to New England in 1997, and has spent the last two decades trying figure out the difference between a hoagie and a sub.

Susan Lerner is a graduate of Butler's MFA in Creative Writing program. She reads for *Creative Nonfiction* and *Booth*, which also published her interview with Jonathan Franzen. Her essay "Only A Memory" was a finalist for the *Crab Orchard Review* 2016 Rafael Torch Literary Nonfiction Award. Her work has appeared in *The Rumpus*, *The Believer Logger*, *Front Porch Journal*, *Literary Mama*, and elsewhere. Follow her on Twitter @susanlitelerner.

Beth Levine is a one-time finalist in *The New Yorker* cartoon caption contest. There are those who say she was robbed in the voting. More at bethlevine.net and @BethLevine75.

Jody Mace's essays have appeared in *Full Grown People*; *Washington Post*; *O, the Oprah Magazine*; *Wondertime*; *Brain*; *Child Magazine*; and many other publications, as well as anthologies. She lives in North Carolina with her husband and two dogs, and is the mother of two grown children. She also writes about music, North Carolina, and sometimes, North Carolina's music.

Michael Martone was born in Fort Wayne, Indiana. He has taught at several universities, including Johns Hopkins, Iowa State, Harvard, Alabama, and Syracuse. He participated in the last major memo war fought with actual paper memoranda before the advent of electronic e-mail. Staples were deployed. The paper generated in that war stacks several inches deep, thick enough to stop a bullet. Martone learned that the "cc:" is the most strategic field of the memo's template, and he is sad to realize that fewer and fewer readers know what the "cc:" stands for, let alone have ever held a piece of the delicate and duplicating artifact in their ink-stained and smudge-smudged fingers. It, like everything else, is history.

Lorri McDole's stories (true, funny, and otherwise) have appeared or are forthcoming in *The Offing; Sweet: A Literary Confection; Cleaver; Eclectica; matchbook; New Madrid; Epiphany;* and *Brain, Child,* as well as in several anthologies. Her essay, "Storms of the Circus World," which was a 2016 finalist for the Talking Writing Prize for Personal Essay, was nominated for a Best of the Net Award. She lives in the Pacific Northwest with her family.

Judy Millar is a Canadian writer, speaker, and comedic storyteller. She's been published in *Reader's Digest* and *Writers' Digest.* She's working on her second book—*Millar Lite: A Comic Look at Life, Love, Sex and Survival.* Judy entertains audiences with hilarious stories based on her life experiences—solo, and as part of the storytelling duo WordChickz. (Judy stresses she's *not* Judith Miller, the Pulitzer-Prize winning journalist who wrote about weapons of mass destruction and went to jail rather than reveal her sources. She'd give up her own grandmother under duress and her Pulitzer is, apparently, still in the mail.) Visit judymillar.ca for more.

Damhnait Monaghan is a Canadian now living in the UK. Her flash fiction has placed in several competitions and last year won the *Brilliant Flash Fiction* "Special Delivery" competition. Her stories, real and imagined, are published in places like *Understorey Magazine, Still Point Arts Quarterly, A Box of Stars Beneath the Bed* (the 2016 National Flash Fiction Day Anthology), *Flash Frontier, Spelk Fiction, The Fiction Pool,* and *Ellipsis Zine.* She's on Twitter @ Downith (which is also how to pronounce her first name.)

Dinty W. Moore is author of *The Rose Metal Press Field Guide to Writing Flash Nonfiction, Crafting the Personal Essay,* and the memoir *Between Panic & Desire.* Moore lives in Athens, Ohio, frightened the great writer and editor George Plimpton on more than one occasion, and is deathly afraid of polar bears.

Chris Offutt is the author of six books, ten screenplays, and two jokes. His nonfiction includes three memoirs: *The Same River Twice, No Heroes,* and *My Father, the Pornographer.* His essays have appeared in a number of magazines and anthologies, including *Pushcart Prize, 2017* and *Best American Essays.* He has a humorous nonfiction cooking column in the quarterly magazine *Oxford American*. His new book, *Country Dark*, is out in April 2018. He grew up in the hills of eastern Kentucky and lives in Mississippi. He is at work on a third joke.

Diane Payne's most recent publications include pieces in *Obra/Artiface, Reservoir, Spry Literary Review, Watershed Review, Superstition Review, Tishman Review, Whiskey Island, Kudzu House Quarterly, Superstition Review, Blue Lyra Press, Fourth River, Cheat River Review, The Offing, Elke: A little Journal, Souvenir Literary Journal, Reservoir,* and *Outpost 19*. Diane is the author of *Burning Tulips* (Red Hen Press) and coauthor of *Delphi Series 5* chapbook.

Meg Pokrass is the author of four collections of flash fiction, and one award-winning collection of prose poetry, *Cellulose Pajamas*, which received the Bluelight Book Award in 2016. Her stories and poems have been widely published and anthologized in two Norton anthologies: *Flash Fiction International* (W. W. Norton & Company; 2015) and the forthcoming *New Micro* (W. W. Norton & Company, 2018). Meg is the founder of *New Flash Fiction Review*, cofounder of The Flash Fiction Collective in San Francisco, and currently serves as festival curator for the Bath Flash Fiction Festival, UK.

Charles Rafferty's twelfth collection of poems is *The Smoke of Horses* (BOA Editions; 2017). His poems have appeared in *The New Yorker; O, the Oprah Magazine; Prairie Schooner;* and *Ploughshares;* and his stories have appeared in *The Southern Review* and *Per Contra*. His stories have been collected in *Saturday Night at Magellan's*. He has won the 2016 NANO Fiction prize, as well as grants from the National Endowment for the Arts and the Connecticut Commission on Culture and Tourism. Currently, he directs the MFA program at Albertus Magnus College.

Lisa Romeo is the author of *Starting with Goodbye: A Daughter's Memoir of Love after Loss* (University of Nevada Press; May 2018). She is part of the faculty of the Bay Path University MFA program, and has taught at several universities in New Jersey. Her work is listed in *Best American Essays 2016*, and appears in popular and literary media, including the *New York Times; O, the*

Oprah Magazine; Inside Jersey; Brevity; Hippocampus; Under the Sun; and others. A former equestrian journalist and public relations specialist, Lisa now works as a freelance manuscript editor, ghostwriter, and writing coach. She lives in New Jersey with her husband and sons.

Mark Rooke was born in Atlanta, Georgia. His writing focuses on humor that unpacks the unpleasantries of life, spins them around, and points out that anything can be ridiculous if you look at it the right way. He currently lives in San Francisco, where his hobbies include complaining about the rising cost of tea and abusing rental cars.

Josh Russell has published three novels and more than eighty stories and essays. His work has earned him a National Endowment for the Arts fellowship and has appeared in *One Story, Subtropics, Epoch, Cincinnati Review, Okey-Panky,* and the anthology *New Microfiction.* He lives in Decatur, Georgia.

Thaddeus Rutkowski is the author of the books *Guess and Check, Violent Outbursts, Haywire, Tetched,* and *Roughhouse. Haywire* won the Members' Choice Award given by the Asian American Writers Workshop. He teaches at Sarah Lawrence College, Medgar Evers College, and the Writer's Voice of the West Side YMCA in New York. He received a fiction writing fellowship from the New York Foundation for the Arts.

Scott Loring Sanders is the author of two novels, a short story collection, and a memoir/essay collection, *Surviving Jersey: Danger & Insanity in the Garden State.* His essays have appeared in such journals as *Creative Nonfiction, North American Review, Sweet,* and many others, and have been noted in *Best American Essays.* His fiction has been included in *Best American Mystery Stories,* and widely published and anthologized. He's been a fellow at the Camargo Foundation in Cassis, France; at the Edward F. Albee Foundation; and at the Virginia Center for the Creative Arts. He teaches at Emerson College and Lesley University. To learn more, go to www.scottloringsanders.com.

Candy Schulman's humor and personal essays have appeared in the *New York Times, Washington Post, Chicago Tribune, McSweeney's, Rumpus Funny*

Women, Salon, among others. Her work has won awards from the American Society of Journalists and Authors, and has received notable recognition in *Best American Essays.* She lives in Greenwich Village, drinks too much coffee, and is a writing professor at The New School. She wishes she had written this quote but Tina Fey got to it first: "Confidence is 10 percent hard work and 90 percent delusion."

Leta McCollough Seletzky is a recovering litigator whose work has appeared in *OZY* and *The Manifest-Station.* She is writing a father-daughter memoir in the Djerassi Resident Artists Program's yearlong Writing Your Book-Length Narrative workshop.

Ravi Shankar is author/editor of a dozen books, including most recently *The Golden Shovel: New Poems Honoring Gwendolyn Brooks* and *Autobiography of a Goddess,* translations of the ninth-century Tamil poet/saint, Andal. He founded the online journal of arts *Drunken Boat,* has won a Pushcart Prize and a RISCA artist grant, has appeared in the *New York Times, Paris Review,* on NPR, the BBC, and PBS, and been interviewed and translated into over ten languages.

Amy Shaw is a creative nonfiction writer who focuses her writing in the areas of personal essay, memoir, biography, and poetry. She is pursuing an MFA in writing from Bay Path University. She is a graduate of Wheaton College (BA), UNC-CH (MLS), and Bay Path University (EdS). Amy has previously worked at the *Berkshire Eagle* and *Washington Post.* She lives in the Berkshire Hills of Massachusetts and teaches social studies to students in grades 7 through 12. A firm believer in the power of belly laughs, dark chocolate, and one's inner rock star, Amy shares her insights and life drama on her blog, ashawwriter.blogspot. com.

Jim Shea is a former humor columnist for the *Hartford Courant.* He now writes a weekly humor column for the Hearst Media Group, which is the largest newspaper chain in Connecticut. He lives on the shoreline with his wife and untrainable dog, and is working on his first novel.

Suzanne Strempek Shea's twelve books include the novel *Hoopi Shoopi Donna*, the story of a woman who honors her late father's wish that she start an all-girl accordion band and make a killing at weddings. When not busy playing hits including "Who Stole the Kiszka," main character, Donna Milewski, works at a tampon factory inspired by the one in Suzanne's essay for this book. A former newspaper reporter, Suzanne has freelanced for publications including the *Boston Globe, Yankee, Irish Times, Down East, Golf World*, and *ESPN the Magazine*. She teaches in the Stonecoast MFA program, is writer-in-residence at Bay Path University, and has led workshops throughout the United States and in Ireland.

Rebecca Van Horn has previously been published in *Quarterly West, The Atticus Review, Moment Magazine*, and *Outlook Springs*, among others. In 2016 she was nominated for a Pushcart Prize. She recently graduated with an MFA in Creative Nonfiction from the University of New Hampshire.

Thomas Jeffrey Vasseur is a native of Kentucky and graduated from Transylvania University, then earned his PhD from the University of Utah. He has published work in *Pleiades, New Mexico Humanities Review, Quarterly West, Other Voices*, and other literary magazines. His short-short "Theology" appeared in *Sudden Flash Youth: 65 Short-Short Stories*. His full-length books are *Touch the Earth: An Aftermath of the Vietnam War*, and the short story collection *Discovering the World: Thirteen Stories*. He teaches at Valdosta State University and lives in St. Augustine.

Anna Vodicka's essays have appeared in a variety of magazines and anthologies, including *AFAR, Brevity, Guernica, Harvard Review, Iowa Review, Longreads, McSweeney's Internet Tendency, Ninth Letter, Paste*, and Lonely Planet's *An Innocent Abroad*. She has won the *Missouri Review* audio competition for prose, earned Pushcart Prize Special Mention, notables in *Best American Essays* and *Best American Travel Writing*, and residency fellowships at Vermont Studio Center and Hedgebrook. She currently writes from Seattle, where she teaches flash nonfiction at the Hugo House and the King County Jail.

Sarah Broussard Weaver is an MFA candidate at Rainier Writing Workshop. Her essays have been published in *Full Grown People, Hippocampus, The Nervous Breakdown,* and *The Bitter Southerner,* among other publications. She lives in Portland, Oregon.

Allison K. Williams has written about race, culture, and comedy for National Public Radio, Canadian Broadcasting Corporation, *New York Times, Christian Science Monitor, McSweeney's Internet Tendency,* and *Travelers' Tales.* Her essays have appeared in *Kenyon Review Online, Prairie Schooner, The Drum,* and *Brevity.* Her humor writing was a Mark Twain Award winner; she has been twice nominated for a Pushcart Prize. Allison is the Social Media Editor at *Brevity,* and the host of the Brevity Podcast. Find her on Twitter and Instagram @ guerillamemoir, and on her website at www.idowords.net.

Leah Williams, a graduate of the University of Iowa's Nonfiction Writing Program, teaches composition and creative nonfiction at the University of New Hampshire. Her essays have been published in *Brevity* and *Redivider,* and aired on an NPR affiliate. You can find her classic film posts at carygrantwonteatyou. com. She regularly questions her intelligence for continuing to eat beef despite years of warnings.

Credits

Kim Addonizio: "Cocktail Time" is reprinted from *Bukowski in a Sundress: Confessions from a Writing Life*, Viking/Penguin, © Kim Addonizio, 2016. Used by permission of the author.

Marcia Aldrich: "Self-Portrait: Questionnaire" was previously published in *Bending Genre* blog, October 13, 2013. Reprinted by permission of Marcia Aldrich.

Gina Barreca: "Sex and the Socratic Method" was previously published (as "Sex Talk the Socratic Sicilian Way") in the *Hartford Courant*, November 5, 2014. Reprinted by permission of Gina Barreca.

Paul Beckman: "Nothing Happened" was previously published in *Come! Meet My Family and other stories*, 1995. Reprinted by permission of Paul Beckman.

Chelsea Biondolillo: "An Objective Look at My Seven Graduate School Rejections" was previously published in *McSweeney's Internet Tendency*, 2010. Reprinted by permission of the author.

Sven Birkerts: "Hard-On" was previously published as a private broadside. Reprinted by permission of Sven Birkerts.

Douglass Bourne: "Bridge Metaphors Used During the Meeting with Department Heads" was originally published (as "Bridge Metaphors Used During the English Department Meeting with the Dean") in *McSweeney's Internet Tendency*, May 17, 2017. Reprinted by permission of Douglass Bourne.

Caitlin Brady: "When the GOP Takes Away My Birth Control, How Will I Know What Day It Is?" was previously published in *McSweeney's Internet Tendency*. Reprinted by permission of *McSweeney's Internet Tendency*.

Wendy Brenner: "For a Friend Who Has Deactivated Her Facebook Account" was previously published in *A Book of Uncommon Prayer,* Outpost 19, San Francisco, 2015. Reprinted by permission of Wendy Brenner.

Dani Burlison: "An Open Letter to Future Ex-Boyfriends About How to Apologize for Wrongdoings at the End of Our Relationship" was previously published at McSweeneys.net. Reprinted by permission of *McSweeney's Internet Tendency.*

Liane Kupferberg Carter: "Gadget Graveyard" was previously published in *Humor Times,* February 2014. Reprinted by permission of Liane Kupferberg Carter.

Josh Couvares: "Pillars of the Community" was previously published in the *Hartford Courant.* Reprinted by permission of the *Hartford Courant.*

Billy Cowan: "The Troubles" was previously published in *Flash: The International Short Short Story Magazine,* Vol. 9. No. 2 (October 2016). Reprinted by permission of Billy Cowan.

Helena de Bres: "Writing Advice to My Students that Would Also Have Been Good Sex Advice for My High School Boyfriends" was previously published in *McSweeney's Internet Tendency,* June 15, 2017. Reprinted by permission of Helena de Bres.

Terri Favro: "Inner Nonna" was previously published in *MORE Magazine* (Canada), September 2007. Reprinted by permission of Terri Favro.

Kathryn Fitzpatrick: "An Angry Letter to Starbucks" was previously published in *Blue Muse Magazine,* April 2017. Reprinted by permission of *Blue Muse Magazine.*

Denis Horgan: A version of "Throw Them Off the Train" was previously published in the *Bangkok World,* copyright 2014. Reprinted by permission of Denis Horgan.

Dani Johannesen: "Intro to Creative Writing" was previously published in *Brevity,* issue 34, September 2010. Reprinted by permission of Dani Johannesen.

Jenny Klion: "Jobs, A to Z" was previously published in *The Villager,* July 2014. Reprinted by permission of Jenny Klion.

Fiona Tinwei Lam: "Nipples" was previously published as part of "Body Tales" in *Ricepaper Magazine*, Issue 20:2, Summer 2015; and subsequently reprinted in *Boobs: Women Explore What It Means to Have Breasts*, edited by Ruth Daniell (Caitlin Press, Canada: 2016). All rights remain with the author. Reprinted by permission of Fiona Tinwei Lam.

Sandra Gail Lambert: "Horror in the Okefenokee Swamp" was previously published in *Breath and Shadow: A Journal of Disability Culture and Literature*, vol. 4, #7, 2007. It will appear in *A Certain Loneliness: A Memoir* (University of Nebraska Press: 2018). Reprinted by permission of the University of Nebraska Press.

Sarah Wesley Lemire: "The Bad Passenger" was previously published in the *Hartford Courant*. Reprinted by permission of the *Hartford Courant*.

Beth Levine: "The Tao of Weighing In" was previously published in the *Chicago Tribune*, September 1, 2004. Reprinted by permission of Beth Levine.

Jody Mace: "The Insomniac's To-Do List" was previously published on FullGrownPeople.com in September 2013. Reprinted by permission of Jody Mace.

Michael Martone: "A Contributor's Note" was previously published in *Booth* #4. Reprinted by permission of Michael Martone.

Lorri McDole: "Bride of Christ" was previously published in *Eclectica*, Oct/Nov 2007. Reprinted by permission of Lorri McDole.

Dinty W. Moore: "Free Tibet, Man!" was previously published in *Brevity*, Issue 2, 1998. Reprinted by permission of the author.

Diane Payne: "How I Ended Up Nearly Bald" was previously published in *Story South*, Spring 2015. Reprinted by permission of Diane Payne.

Lisa Romeo: "The Long Pink Line" was previously published online at Erma Bombeck's Writers' Workshop (HumorWriters.org). Reprinted by permission of Lisa Romeo.

Mark Rooke: "Before We Break for Lunch, Let Me Repeat Everything Already Said at This Meeting At Least Twice" was previously published in *McSweeney's Internet Tendency* on September 8, 2015. Reprinted by permission of Mark Rooke.

CPSIA information can be obtained
at www.ICGtesting.com
Printed in the USA
LVHW092334210719
624814LV00001B/203/P

9 780997 543742